Fodor's InFocus

FLORIDA KEYS

2nd Edition

Where to Stay and Eat
for All Budgets

Must-See Sights
and Local Secrets

Ratings You Can Trust

Excerpted from *Fodor's Florida*

Fodor's Travel Publications New York, Toronto, London, Sydney, Auckland

www.fodors.com

FODOR'S IN FOCUS FLORIDA KEYS

Series Editor: Douglas Stallings

Editor: Carolyn Galgano

Editorial Production: Carolyn Roth

Editorial Contributors: Chelle Koster Walton, Teri Evans, and Michael de Zayas

Maps & Illustrations: David Lindroth, *cartographer*; Bob Blake and Rebecca Baer, *map editors*; William Wu, *information graphics*

Design: Fabrizio LaRocca, *creative director*; Guido Caroti, *art director*; Ann McBride, *designer*; Melanie Marin, *senior picture editor*

Cover Photo: (Key West Lighthouse) Mark Lewis/Digital Vision/Getty Images

Production/Manufacturing: Amanda Bullock

COPYRIGHT

2nd Edition

ISBN 978-1-4000-0507-9

ISSN 1942-7328

SPECIAL SALES

This book is available for special discounts for bulk purchases for sales promotions or premiums. Special editions, including personalized covers, excerpts of existing books, and corporate imprints, can be created in large quantities for special needs. For more information, write to Special Markets/Premium Sales, 1745 Broadway, MD 6-2, New York, NY 10019, or e-mail specialmarkets@randomhouse.com.

AN IMPORTANT TIP & AN INVITATION

Although all prices, opening times, and other details in this book are based on information supplied to us at press time, changes occur all the time in the travel world, and Fodor's cannot accept responsibility for facts that become outdated or for inadvertent errors or omissions. **So always confirm information when it matters,** especially if you're making a detour to visit a specific place. Your experiences—positive and negative—matter to us. If we have missed or misstated something, **please write to us.** We follow up on all suggestions. Contact the Florida Keys editor at editors@fodors.com or c/o Fodor's at 1745 Broadway, New York, NY 10019.

PRINTED IN THE UNITED STATES OF AMERICA

10 9 8 7 6 5 4 3 2

Be a Fodor's Correspondent

Your opinion matters. It matters to us. It matters to your fellow Fodor's travelers, too. And we'd like to hear it. In fact, we *need* to hear it. When you share your experiences and opinions, you become an active member of the Fodor's community. Here's how you can help improve Fodor's for all of us.

Tell us when we're right. We rely on local writers to give you an insider's perspective. But our writers and staff editors also depend on you. Your positive feedback is a vote to renew our recommendations for the next edition.

Tell us when we're wrong. We update most of our guides every year. But things change. If any of our descriptions are inaccurate or inadequate, we'll incorporate your changes in the next edition and will correct factual errors at fodors.com *immediately*.

Tell us what to include. You probably have had fantastic travel experiences that aren't yet in Fodor's. Why not share them with a community of like-minded travelers? Share your discoveries and experiences with everyone directly at fodors.com. Your input may lead us to add a new listing or a higher recommendation.

Give us your opinion instantly at our feedback center at www.fodors.com/feedback. You may also e-mail editors@fodors.com with the subject line "Florida Keys Editor." Or send your nominations, comments, and complaints by mail to Florida Keys Editor, Fodor's, 1745 Broadway, New York, NY 10019.

Happy Traveling!

Tim Jarrell, Publisher

CONTENTS

MAPS

ABOUT THIS BOOK

Our Ratings

We wouldn't recommend a place that wasn't worth your time, but sometimes a place is so experiential that superlatives don't do it justice: you just have to be there to know. These sights, properties, and experiences get our highest rating, **Fodor's Choice**, indicated by orange stars throughout this book. Black stars highlight sights and properties we deem **Highly Recommended**, places that our writers, editors, and readers praise again and again for consistency and excellence.

Credit Cards

Want to pay with plastic? **AE, D, DC, MC, V** after restaurant and hotel listings indicate whether American Express, Discover, Diners Club, MasterCard, and Visa are accepted.

Restaurants

Unless we state otherwise, restaurants are open for lunch and dinner daily. We mention dress only when there's a specific requirement and reservations only when they're essential or not accepted—it's always best to book ahead.

Hotels

Unless we tell you otherwise, you can assume that the hotels have private bath, phone, TV, and air-conditioning. We always list facilities but not whether you'll be charged an extra fee to use them, so when pricing accommodations, find out what's included.

Many Listings
- ★ Fodor's Choice
- ★ Highly recommended
- ✉ Physical address
- ✛ Directions
- ⌂ Mailing address
- ☎ Telephone
- 🖷 Fax
- ⊕ On the Web
- ✍ E-mail
- 🎫 Admission fee
- ☉ Open/closed times
- Ⓜ Metro stations
- ▭ Credit cards

Hotels & Restaurants
- 🏨 Hotel
- ⇦ Number of rooms
- ☖ Facilities
- ⦿ Meal plans
- W Restaurant
- ⟁ Reservations
- ↘ Smoking
- ⅋ BYOB
- ✕🏨 Hotel with restaurant that warrants a visit

Outdoors
- ⚐ Golf
- ⛺ Camping

Other
- ☃ Family-friendly
- ⇨ See also
- ✉ Branch address
- ☞ Take note

WHEN TO GO

High season in the Keys is mid-December through mid-April, and traffic on the Overseas Highway is inevitably heavy. From November to the middle of December, crowds are thinner, the weather is superlative, and hotels and shops drastically reduce their prices. Summer, which is hot and humid, is becoming a second high season, especially among families, Europeans, bargain-seekers, and lobster divers. (Rooms are scarce the first few weekends of lobster season, which starts in early August and runs through March.) There's also a two-day sport season in late July. Key West's annual Fantasy Fest is the last week in October; if you plan to attend this wildly popular event (emphasis on wild), reserve at least six months in advance. In Key Largo, room availability and rates are often affected by races at the Miami Homestead Speedway.

Climate

Florida is rightly called the Sunshine State. (Areas like Tampa Bay report 361 days of sunshine a year!) But it could also be dubbed the Humid State. From June through September, 90% humidity levels are not uncommon. Thankfully, the weather in the Keys is more moderate than in mainland Florida. Temperatures can be 10°F cooler during the summer and up to 10°F warmer during the winter. The Keys also get substantially less rain

than mainland Florida—around 30 inches annually, compared with an average 55 to 60 inches in Miami and the Everglades. Most rain falls in quick downpours on summer afternoons, except in June, September, and October, when tropical storms can dump rain for two to four days. Winter cold fronts occasionally stall over the Keys, dragging overnight temperatures down to the high 40s. The hurricane season, which runs from June through November, can put a crimp on a summer or fall vacation. The Keys get their fair share of watches, warnings, and evacuation notices. Pay heed and evacuate earlier rather than later, when flights and automobile traffic get backed up.

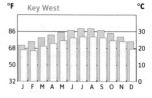

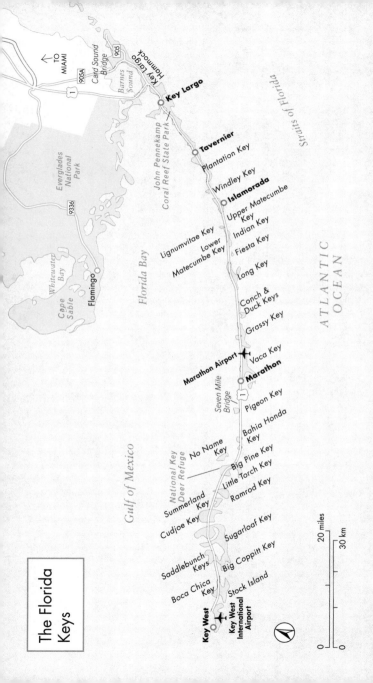

The Florida Keys

← TO MIAMI

Card Sound Bridge

905A

1

905

Barnes Sound

Key Largo Hammock

Key Largo

John Pennekamp Coral Reef State Park

Tavernier

Plantation Key

Windley Key

Islamorada

Upper Matecumbe Key

Lignumvitae Key

Indian Key

Lower Matecumbe Key

Fiesta Key

Long Key

Conch & Duck Keys

Grassy Key

Marathon Airport

Vaca Key

Marathon

1

Seven Mile Bridge

Pigeon Key

Bahia Honda Key

No Name Key

National Key Deer Refuge

Big Pine Key

Little Torch Key

Summerland Key

Ramrod Key

Cudjoe Key

Sugarloaf Key

Saddlebunch Keys

Big Coppitt Key

Boca Chica Key

Stock Island

Key West

Key West International Airport

Everglades National Park

9336

Whitewater Bay

Flamingo

Cape Sable

Florida Bay

Gulf of Mexico

Straits of Florida

ATLANTIC OCEAN

20 miles

30 km

0

0

Welcome to the Florida Keys

WORD OF MOUTH

"The beauty of Key West is that if you stay in Old Town, everything you want to do (including sunset celebrations, restaurants, water sports and other tourist activities) will be within walking distance."

—SusanCS

"Marathon is a great little place. Lots of inexpensive, interesting places to eat and it is a short drive to Key West."

—islandgirl355

By Chelle
Koster
Walton

BEING A CONCH is a condition of the heart, and foreclosure on the soul. Many throughout the Florida Keys wear that label proudly, yet there is anything but a shared lifestyle here. To the south, Key West has a Mardi Gras mood with Fantasy Festivals, Hemingway look-alike contests, and the occasional threat to secede from the Union. It's an island whose melting-pot character allows crusty natives to mingle (more or less peacefully) with eccentrics and escape artists who lovingly call this 4-mi sandbar "Paradise." Although life elsewhere in the island chain isn't quite as offbeat, it's nearly as diverse.

Flowering jungles, shimmering seas, and mangrove-lined islands are also, conversely, overburdened. A river of tourist traffic gushes along U.S. 1 (also called the Overseas Highway), the 110-mi artery linking the inhabited islands. Residents of Monroe County live by diverting the river's flow of dollars to their own pockets. In the process, the fragile beauty of the Keys—or at least the 45 that are inhabited and linked to the mainland by 42 bridges—is paying an environmental price.

At the top, nearest the mainland, is Key Largo, becoming more congested as it evolves into a bedroom community and weekend hideaway for residents of Miami and Fort Lauderdale. At the bottom, 106 mi southwest, is Key West, where hundreds of passengers from multiple cruise ships swarm the narrow streets. Offshore is the Florida Keys National Marine Sanctuary, established by Congress in 1990, a wondrous but fragile environment of sea-grass meadows, mangrove islands, and living coral reefs.

The expansion of U.S. 1 to the mainland to four lanes will open the floodgates to increased traffic, population, and tourism. For now, however, take pleasure as you drive down U.S. 1 along the islands. Gaze over the silvery blue-and-green Atlantic and its still-living reef, with Florida Bay, the Gulf of Mexico, and the backcountry on your right (the Keys extend east–west from the mainland).

At a few points the ocean and Gulf are as much as 10 mi apart. In most places, however, they are from 1 to 4 mi apart, and on the narrowest landfill islands they are separated only by the road. Try to get off the highway. Once you do, rent a boat, anchor, and then fish, swim, or marvel at the sun, sea, and sky. In the Atlantic, dive spectacular coral reefs or pursue grouper, blue marlin, and other deepwater game fish. Along Florida Bay's coastline, kayak and canoe

1

to secluded islands and bays or seek out the bonefish, snapper, snook, and tarpon that lurk in the grass flats and in the shallow, winding channels of the backcountry.

WHAT'S WHERE

The Florida Keys are the dribble of islands off the peninsula's southern tip. From Miami International Airport, Key Largo is a 56-mi drive along the Overseas Highway. The rest of the Keys—Islamorada, Marathon, Bahia Honda Key, Big Pine Key—fall in succession for the 106 mi between Key Largo and Key West. At their north end the Florida Keys front Florida Bay, which separates it from Everglades National Park. The Middle and Lower Keys front the Gulf of Mexico; the Atlantic Ocean borders the length of the chain on its eastern shores.

The Upper Keys. As the doorstep to the islands' coral reefs and blithe spirit, the Upper Keys introduce all that is sporting and sea-oriented about the Keys. They stretch from Key Largo to the Long Key Channel (MM 106–65).

The Middle Keys. Centered around the town of Marathon, the Middle Keys hold most of the chain's historic and natural attractions outside of Key West. They go from Conch (pronounced *konk*) Key through Marathon to the south side of the Seven Mile Bridge, including Pigeon Key (MM 65–40).

The Lower Keys. Pressure drops another notch in this laidback part of the region, where wildlife and the fishing lifestyle peak. The Lower Keys go from Little Duck Key south through Big Coppitt Key (MM 40–9).

Key West. The ultimate in Florida Keys craziness, the party town Key West isn't the place for those seeking a quiet retreat. The Key West area encompasses MM 9–0.

THE MILEMARKER SYSTEM

Getting lost in the Keys is almost impossible once you understand the unique address system. **Many addresses are simply given as a mile marker (MM) number.** The markers are small, green, rectangular signs along the side of the Overseas Highway (U.S. 1). They begin with MM 126, 1 mi south of Florida City, and end with MM 0, in Key West. **Keys residents use the abbreviation BS for the bay side of Overseas Highway and OS for the ocean side.** From Marathon to Key West, residents may refer to the bay side as the gulf side.

HISTORY OF THE KEYS

One thing persists throughout the history of the Florida Keys: change. Of course every destination evolves and matures, but the mood swings in the Keys seem singularly drastic. Except for Key West, an important shipping way station since Florida's earliest days, the Keys were only sparsely populated until the early 20th century.

The first residents were the Calusa and the Tequesta tribes, whose parched skeletons earned Key West its original Spanish name, Cayo Hueso (Bone Key). Ponce de León led the Spanish invasion after discovering the Keys on his first voyage in 1513, labeling the chain Les Martires because from the distance they appeared as men in distress, perhaps martyrs.

Despite their strategic shipping position, the Keys did indeed make martyrs of many ships that collided with the tricky barrier reef. Thus began one the most lucrative industries in the history of the Keys: salvaging shipwrecks. The occupation brought the first influx of white Bahamians—descendants of Loyalists who had fled to the islands after the American Revolution. Wrecking turned Key West into the richest city in the Americas (and largest in Florida), but that changed suddenly and drastically with the building of lighthouses.

Once the Keys became part of the United States and the Navy moved into Key West, an end came to another under-the-radar occupation, namely pirating. From feast to famine, islanders found new ways to scrape out a living. Next on the less-than-legal agenda was poaching birds for their feathers, until their decimation led to outcry, legislation, and enforcement. Rum-running and later drug smuggling continued the Keys' reputation for renegade lawlessness. Other islanders turned to fishing, sponging, and farming to eke out a meager existence.

In Key West, Cuban dissidents brought cigar-making to the economy in the 1860s, but aside from that, jobs were otherwise scarce until 1905. That was the year railroad magnate Henry Flagler began building the extension of his Florida railroad south from Homestead to Key West, despite ridicule and against all odds. His goal was to establish a Miami–Key West rail link for his steamships that sailed between Key West and Havana, just 90 mi across the Straits of Florida.

1

The monumental undertaking required tons of manpower, especially because the work was so intense and conditions so unhealthy that many lost their lives in the endeavor. Flagler bulked his work force with Bahamian immigrants and drifters from the South, and the town of Marathon swelled into an unruly, liquor-lubricated town, fueled by one of the largest payrolls in Florida at the time. The railroad arrived at Key West in 1912, and remained a lifeline of commerce until the Labor Day hurricane of 1935 washed out much of its roadbed. Along with it, the hurricane wiped out pineapple farming, and once again residents found themselves destitute. The Overseas Highway, built over the railroad's old roadbeds and bridges, was completed in 1938. With it came a pipeline bringing water from Miami and modern conveniences for the Navy and inhabitants.

The new highway brought tourists eager to view the Keys' pristine coral reefs and pull fish from the great schools that gathered around them. The dedication of Everglades National Park, John Pennekamp Coral Reef State Park, and National Key Deer Refuge increased environmental awareness. Hurricanes continued to impede prosperity, however. Only in modern times has tourism grown to fully sustain the Keys, but this sweet story has its own bitter side as scientists see the effect of car fumes and runoff killing the very environment that attracts visitors. As the federal government works to restore destruction in neighboring Everglades National Park, local agencies push for reef relief. Hopefully heightened awareness will save the Keys from further irreparable environmental damage. Luckily, major hurricanes have missed the Keys for quite some time. Key Westers attribute it to the outdoor shrine at St. Mary Star of the Sea Catholic Church, where they come to pray and light candles when tropical storms threaten.

NATURE IN THE KEYS

More than 600 varieties of fish populate the reefs and islands of the Florida Keys. Diminutive Key deer and skinny raccoons, related to but distinct from their mainland cousins, inhabit the Lower Keys. And throughout the islands you'll find such exotic West Indian plants as Jamaican dogwood, lignumvitae, pigeon plum, poisonwood, satin leaf, and silver thatch palms, as well as subtropical birds, including the great white heron, mangrove cuckoo, roseate spoonbill, and white-crowned pigeon. Mangroves,

CLOSE UP

Going Buggy over Lobster

They call them "bug-hunters," and they descend in swarms. Lobster divers come in quest of the coveted Florida lobster, aka "bug," each year during sport season, the last consecutive Wednesday and Thursday in July, and regular season (early August through March), when they must compete against commercial operations. The clawless spiny lobster is taken for its tail meat, which some proclaim sweeter than Maine lobster meat. Harvesting regulations are strict, and all divers must carry a special gauge to make sure their catch has a carapace longer than 3 inches and a tail longer than 5½ inches. Bag limit is six legal lobsters per harvester per day. Diving for lobsters at night (one hour after official sunset and one hour before sunrise) is prohibited. Harvesting in John Pennekamp Coral Reef State Park and other designated areas is also prohibited. For more information, visit ⊕ www.fla-keys.com/diving/lobster.htm.

with their gracefully bowed prop roots, appear to march out to sea. Day by day they busily add more keys to the archipelago.

With virtually no distracting air pollution or obstructive high-rises, sunsets are a pure, unadulterated spectacle that each evening attracts thousands to waterfront parks, piers, restaurants, bars, and resorts throughout the Keys. Weather is another attraction: winter is typically 10°F warmer than on the mainland; summer is usually 10°F cooler. The Keys also get substantially less rain, around 30 inches annually, compared with an average 55 to 60 inches in Miami and the Everglades. Most rain falls in quick downpours on summer afternoons, except in June, September, and October, when tropical storms can dump rain for two to four days. Winter cold fronts occasionally stall over the Keys, dragging overnight temperatures down to the high 40s.

While the living reef surrounding the Keys has been in decline since the early 1980s, scientists have recognized that the larger ecosystem must be preserved in order to ensure the reef's continued health. In 1990 Congress established the Florida Keys National Marine Sanctuary to protect the wondrous but fragile environment of sea-grass meadows, mangrove islands, and living coral reefs that surrounds the Keys. Its primary purpose is to enforce a comprehensive

Croc Territory

CLOSE UP

1

If you take Card Sound Road to get from the mainland to Key Largo (rather than U.S. 1), you'll travel through off-the-beaten-path Florida, including **Crocodile Lake National Wildlife Refuge**. Home to North America's largest concentration of saltwater crocs, it has no public access except by water. These crocodiles are normally shy, but sometimes you can see them sunning on the shore, their mouths opened menacingly to keep cool. You can tell you're looking at a crocodile, not an alligator, if you can see its lower teeth protruding when its jaws are shut. Gators are much darker in color—a grayish black—compared with the lighter tan color of crocodiles. Alligators' snouts are also much broader than their long, thin crocodilian counterparts. Open to the public is an interpretive **butterfly garden** next to refuge headquarters at Mile Marker 106. Adjacent to it lies **Dagny Johnson Key Largo Hammocks State Park** with a self-guided nature trail and similar species to Crocodile Lake NWR.

program to protect the ecosystem, which is being compromised by pollution, overuse, and rising sea temperatures.

IF YOU LIKE

BOATING

If it floats, local marinas rent it. For up-close exploration of the mangroves and near-shore islands in Florida Bay, nothing beats a kayak or canoe or the latest innovation, standup paddling on a surfboard. Whichever you choose, you are often able to paddle within a few feet of a flock of birds without disturbing it. Visiting the backcountry islands and inlets of Everglades National Park requires a shallow-draft boat: a 14- to 17-foot skiff with a 40- to 50-horsepower outboard is sufficient. Rental companies prohibit smaller boats from going on the ocean side. For diving the reef or fishing on the open ocean, you'll need a larger boat with greater horsepower. Houseboats are ideal for cruising the Keys near shore. Only experienced sailors should attempt to navigate the shallow waters surrounding the Keys with deep-keeled sailboats. On the other hand, small shallow-draft, single-hull sailboats and catamarans are ideal. Those interested in experiencing the reef without getting wet can take a glass-bottom-boat trip.

FISHING

These sun-bathed waters have many species of game fish as well as lobster, shrimp, and crabs. Flats fishing and backcountry fishing are Keys specialties. In flats fishing a guide poles a shallow-draft outboard boat through the skinny, sandy-bottom waters while sighting for bonefish and snook to catch on light tackle, spin, and fly. Backcountry fishing may include flats fishing or fishing in the channels and basins around islands in Florida Bay. Charter boats fish the reef and Gulf Stream for deep-sea fish. Party boats, which can be crowded, carry up to 50 people to fish the reefs for grouper, kingfish, and snapper. Some operators have a guarantee, or NO FISH, NO PAY policy. It's customary to tip the crew 15% to 20% of the trip price if they were helpful. The best places to station a fishing vacation are Islamorada and Big Pine Key.

SCUBA DIVING AND SNORKELING

Diving in the Keys is spectacular. In shallow and deep water—with visibility up to 120 feet—you can explore sea canyons and mountains covered with waving sea plumes, brain and star coral, historic shipwrecks, and sunken submarines. The best coral reef diving is just outside the waters of John Pennekamp Coral Reef State Park, in Key Largo, and Looe Key Reef, off Ramrod Key. Avid wreck divers might consider tackling all or part of the **Keys Spanish Galleon Trail** (⊕ *www.flheritage.com/archaeology*).

There's no best season for diving, but occasional storms from June through November cloud the waters and make seas rough. Explore the reefs with scuba, snuba (a cross between scuba and snorkeling), or snorkeling gear, using your own boat or a rented boat or by booking a tour with a dive shop. Tours depart two or three times a day, stopping at one to three sites each trip. The first trip of the day is usually the best. It's less crowded—vacationers like to sleep in—and visibility is better before the wind picks up in the afternoon.

There's also night diving. If you want to scuba dive but are not certified, take an introductory resort course. Although it doesn't result in certification, it allows you to dive with an instructor in the afternoon after morning classroom and pool instruction. Most dive shops also offer full certification courses. To save time, you can begin the course at home and save your certification dives for the warm, hospitable Keys waters. Nearly all the waters surrounding the Keys are part of the Florida Keys National Marine Sanctuary, and are thus protected; the reef is fragile and shouldn't be touched.

NIGHTLIFE

In two words: Key West. Duval Street has been compared to Las Vegas's strip and New Orleans' Bourbon Street for its all-day, all-night party. Locals, cruise-ship passengers, and other visitors do the Duval Crawl, hitting bar after bar known for their margaritas, live bands, and sometimes raunchy activities. Other Keys boast a legendary nightspot or two such as Lorelei's Cabana Bar in Islamorada and the Caribbean Club in Key Largo. Both are colorful in their own peculiar way.

CULTURE

The flip side to Key West's bawdy personality is the number of museums, historic sites, and art galleries it holds. Through the decades, the island has attracted writers and artists, who have bequeathed it a sort of lowdown highbrow legacy. Most of Old Town's buildings have a historical context. Some, such as the Ernest Hemingway's Home and the Harry S. Truman Little House Museum, welcome visitors. Others you can admire from the outside. Museums explore everything from pirates and sunken treasure to fine art and the Cuban heritage. Museums thin out as you head north of Key West, but historic sites in Marathon include Pigeon Key and Crane Point Museum. You'll also find wildlife-inspired art galleries throughout the chain.

BEST BEACHES

Because the Bahama Islands steal the Keys' offshore sand, the region has fewer natural beaches than one might expect. But the ones it does have are award-winning, specifically those at Bahia Honda State Park.

Also, just because a beach is not natural, doesn't mean it should be overlooked. Some of the Keys' public man-made beaches provide solid recreation and sunning options for visitors looking to work on their tan. Many resorts additionally provide their own private beachfronts.

The Keys may not have a surplus of beaches, but one nice perk is the availability of camping on some of them. It's one of many ways to enjoy nature while on the beach. Another is keeping an eye out for sea turtles. April through October female sea turtles lay their eggs in the sand for a nearly two-month period of nesting.

■TIP→ **Don't let pests ruin your day at the beach. To avoid the stings of sea lice, remove your swimsuit and shower thoroughly upon exiting the water. Sand fleas (aka no-see-ums) are tiny insects with big teeth that are most likely to attack in the morning and around sunset.**

LONG KEY STATE PARK

The beach at Long Key State Park at MM 67.5 is a typical Middle Key beach. They are more like sand flats, where low tide reveals the coral bedrock of the ecosystem. Here you can snorkel or fish (bonefishing is quite popular) during the day and then be lulled to sleep by the sound of gentle sea waves if you spend the night camping. (The beach is accessible only to campers.)

SOMBRERO BEACH

Something of a local hangout—especially on weekends, when it can get crowded—Sombrero Beach in Marathon is worth getting off the beaten Overseas Highway path for (exit at MM 50 onto Sombrero Beach Road). Families will find much to do on the man-made coved beach and its grassy green, manicured lawn, playground area, and clear, calm waters. Separate sections also accommodate boaters and windsurfers.

BAHIA HONDA STATE PARK

This state park at MM 37 holds three beaches, all of different character. Sandspur Beach is the most removed from crowds, with long stretches of powdery sands and a campground. Loggerhead Beach is closer to the park's concession area, where you can rent snorkel equipment and kayaks. Like Sandspur, it faces the Atlantic Ocean, but waves are typically wimpy. Near Loggerhead, Calusa Beach on the Gulf side near the marina is popular with families, offering a small and safe swimming venue and picnic facilities, as well as camping.

HIGGS BEACH, KEY WEST

Situated on Atlantic Boulevard, this is as urban as beaches in the Keys get, with lots of amenities, activities, and distractions. Visitors can check out a historic site, eat at a popular beachfront Italian restaurant, rent a kayak, play volleyball or tennis, or at the playground—and all within walking distance of the long sweep of man-made beach and sparkling clear, shallow, and calm water.

CLOSE UP

Which Key for Me?

1

Can't decide where to base your Florida Keys vacation? This guide to the different islands' specialties and reputations may help. Note, however, that you will find fishing, diving, kayaking, birding, and other outdoor pursuits everywhere you travel in the Keys.

■ Diving and Snorkeling: Key Largo has a reputation as "Diving Capital of the World."

■ Fishing: Islamorada is known as "Sportfishing Capital of the World." For fishing on a smaller scale, Big Pine Key is the place.

■ Kayaking: Big Pine Key has the most natural attributes and reputable operations.

■ Camping: Long Key State Park's campground sits on one of the Keys' best beaches. You'll find private campgrounds plentiful throughout the Keys.

■ Beaching: Bahia Honda Key's state park is a real show-off.

■ Birding: Key Largo's proximity to Everglades National Park means stunning populations.

■ Celebrity-spotting: Stars and

statesmen show up regularly in Islamorada to catch the big fish. Key West is another place you can often spot celebs hanging out.

■ Dining: Key West takes top rank there, but Islamorada is no slouch.

■ Nightlife: No competition: Key West by a landslide.

■ Museums and Culture: Again, Key West hands down for its historic sites, museums, architecture, art galleries, and theater scene.

■ Gay Vacations: Key West is famous for its tolerance and enlightened attitude. Gay clubs, resorts, and activities are easy to find.

■ Fantasy Resorts: Key Largo is wealthy, with destination resorts that provide it all. The most fantasy resort of all, however, occupies Little Palm Island, accessible only by boat.

■ Guesthouses: More than 100 bed-and-breakfasts and small inns in Key West welcome guests as though they were family.

ZACHARY TAYLOR HISTORIC STATE PARK

This man-made beach is part of a Civil War–era fort complex at the end of Southard Street, and is arguably the best beach in Key West, with its typically small waves, swaying Australian pines, water-sports rentals, and shaded picnic grounds. It also hosts, from mid-January through mid-April, an alfresco collection of oversize art called Sculpture Key West, which changes annually and showcases artists from across the country.

The Upper Keys

WORD OF MOUTH

"The Casa Morada [in Upper Matecumbe Key] was lovely. It is a boutique hotel one block off U.S. 1, but feels like you are in another world. The staff couldn't have been nicer or more helpful. The room came with a lovely breakfast buffet served on an outdoor terrace down by the water. Bottled water and snacks in the refrigerator in the suite were complimentary."

—theatrelover

Updated
by Chelle
Koster
Walton

DIVING AND SNORKELING RULE IN THE UPPER KEYS, thanks to the tropical coral reef that runs a few miles off the Atlantic coast. Divers of all skill levels benefit from accessible dive sites and an established tourism infrastructure. Fishing is another huge draw, especially around Islamorada, known for its sportfishing in both deep offshore waters and in the backcountry. Offshore islands accessible only by boat are popular destinations for kayakers. In short, if you don't like the water you might get bored here.

Other nature lovers won't feel shortchanged. Within 1½ mi of the bay coast lie the mangrove trees and sandy shores of Everglades National Park, where naturalists lead tours of one of the world's few saltwater forests. Here you'll see endangered manatees, curious dolphins, and other underwater creatures. Although the number of birds has dwindled since John James Audubon captured their beauty on canvas, bird-watchers will find plenty to see, including the rare Everglades snail kite, bald eagles, ospreys, and a colorful array of egrets and herons. At sunset flocks take to the skies as they gather to find their night's roost, adding a swirl of activity to an otherwise quiet time of day.

ORIENTATION AND PLANNING

GETTING ORIENTED

The best way to explore this stretch, or any stretch, of the Florida Keys is by boat. As soon as possible you should jump on any seaworthy vessel to see the view of and from the water. And make sure you veer off the main drag of U.S. 1. Head toward the water, where you'll often find the kind of laid-back restaurants and hotels that define the Keys. John Pennekamp Coral Reef State Park is the region's most popular destination, but it's certainly not the only place to get in touch with nature.

PLANNING

GETTING HERE AND AROUND

Airporter operates scheduled van and bus pick-up service from all Miami International Airport (MIA) baggage areas to wherever you want to go in Key Largo ($50) and Islamorada ($55). Groups of three or more passengers receive discounts. There are three departures daily; reservations are preferred 48 hours in advance. The SuperShuttle charges $165 per passenger for trips from Miami International

TOP REASONS TO GO

■ **Snorkeling.** The best snorkeling spots in these parts are to be found around the awe-inspiring Christ of the Abyss east of John Pennekamp Coral Reef State Park in the Florida Keys National Marine Sanctuary.

■ **Sunsets.** Find a comfortable place to watch the sunset, keeping an eye out for the elusive green flash.

■ **Aquatic Mammals.** Get up close and personal with a dolphin or sea lion at Theater of the Sea or a number of other dolphin attractions.

■ **Boating.** Start with a visit to Robbie's Marina on Lower Matecumbe Key in Islamorada, a salty spot to find everything from fishing charters to kayaking rentals.

■ **Nightlife.** It's not a disco, but you can dance the night away to music by local bands at Lorelei's Cabana Bar.

Airport to the Upper Keys. For trips to the airport, place your request 24 hours in advance.

ESSENTIALS

Transportation Contacts **Airporter** (☎ 305/852–3413 or 800/830–3413). **SuperShuttle** (☎ 305/871–2000 ⊕ www.supershuttle.com).

RESTAURANTS

The Upper Keys are full of low-key eateries where the owner is also the chef and the food is tasty and never too fussy. The one exception is Islamorada, where you'll find more upscale restaurants. Restaurants may close for a two- to four-week vacation during the slow season between early September and mid-November.

HOTELS

In the Upper Keys the accommodations are as varied as they are plentiful. The majority of lodgings are in small, narrow waterfront complexes with efficiencies and one- or two-bedroom units. These places offer dockage and often arrange boating, diving, and fishing excursions. There are also larger resorts with every type of activity imaginable and smaller boutique hotels where the attraction is personalized service. Depending on which way the wind blows and how close the property is to the highway, there may be some noise from U.S. 1. If this is an annoyance for you, ask for a room as far from the traffic as possible. Some properties require two- or three-day minimum stays during holiday and high-season weekends. Conversely, discounts apply for midweek, weekly, and monthly stays. Campgrounds and RV parks with full hookups charge around $50

WHAT IT COSTS				
¢	$	$$	$$$	$$$$
RESTAURANTS				
under $10	$10–$15	$15–$20	$20–$30	over $30
HOTELS				
under $80	$80–$100	$100–$140	$140–$220	over $220

Restaurant prices are per person for a main course at dinner. Hotel prices are for a standard double room, excluding 6% sales tax (more in some counties) and 1%–4% tourist tax.

KEY LARGO

56 mi south of Miami International Airport.

The first of the Upper Keys reachable by car, 30-mi-long Key Largo is the largest island in the chain. Key Largo—named Cayo Largo ("Long Key") by the Spanish—makes a great introduction to the region. This is the gateway to the Keys, and an evening of fresh seafood and views of the sunset on the water will get you in the right state of mind.

The history of Largo reads similar to that of the rest of the Keys: a succession of native people, pirates, wreckers, and developers. The first settlement on Key Largo was named Planter, back in the days of pineapple and later key-lime plantations. For a time it was a convenient shipping port, but when the railroad arrived Planter died on the vine. Today three communities—North Key Largo, Key Largo, and Tavernier—make up the whole of Key Largo.

What's there to do on Key Largo besides gaze at the sunset? Not much if you're not into diving or snorkeling. Nobody comes to Key Largo without visiting John Pennkamp Coral Reef State Park, one of the jewels of the state park system. Water sports enthusiasts head to the adjacent Key Largo National Marine Sanctuary, which encompasses about 190 square mi of coral reefs, sea-grass beds, and mangrove estuaries. If you've never tried diving, Key Largo is the

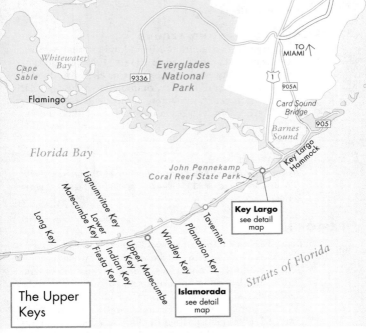

The Upper Keys

perfect place to learn. Dozens of companies will be more than happy to show you the ropes.

Fishing is the other big draw, and world records are broken regularly in the waters around the Upper Keys. There are plenty of charter companies to help you find the big ones and teach you how to hook the elusive bonefish, sometimes known as the ghost fish.

On land, Key Largo offers all the conveniences of a major resort town, including restaurants that will cook your catch or dish up their own offerings with inimitable style. You'll notice that some unusual specialties pop up on the menu, such as cracked conch, spiny lobster, and stone crab. Don't pass up a chance to try the local delicacies, especially the key lime pie.

Most businesses are lined up along U.S. 1, the four-lane highway that runs down the middle of the island. Cars whiz past at all hours—something to remember when you're booking a room. Most lodgings are on the highway, so you'll want to be as far back as possible.

GETTING HERE AND AROUND

Key Largo is 56 mi south of Miami International Airport, the mile markers ranging from 106 to 91. The island runs northeast–southwest, with the Overseas Highway, divided by a median most of the way, running down the center. If the highway is your only glimpse of the island, you're likely to feel barraged by its tacky commercial side. Make a point of driving Route 905 in North Key Largo and down side streets to get a better feel for it.

ESSENTIALS

Visitor Information **Key Largo Chamber of Commerce** (✉ *MM 106 BS, Key Largo* ☎ *305/451–4747 or 800/822–1088* ⊕ *www. keylargochamber.org*).

EXPLORING

Dagny Johnson Key Largo Hammock Botanical State Park. American crocodiles, mangrove cuckoos, white-crowned pigeons, Schaus swallowtail butterflies, mahogany mistletoe, wild cotton, and 100 other rare critters and plants inhabit these 2,400 acres, sandwiched between Crocodile Lake National Wildlife Refuge and Pennekamp Coral Reef State Park. The park is also a user-friendly place to explore the largest remaining stand of the vast West Indian tropical hardwood hammock and mangrove wetland that once covered most of the Keys' upland areas. Interpretive signs describe many of the tropical tree species along a wide 1-mi paved road (2-mi round-trip) that invites walking and biking. There are also more than 6 mi of nature trails accessible to bikes and wheelchairs. Pets are welcome if on a leash no longer than 6 feet. You'll also find restrooms, information kiosks, and picnic tables. ✉ *0.5 mi north of Overseas Hwy. on Rte. 905 OS, North Key Largo* ☎ *305/451–1202* ⊕ *www.floridastateparks.org/keylargohammock* ✍ *$2.50* ☉ *Daily 8–sundown*.

Florida Keys Wild Bird Center. Have a nose-to-beak encounter with ospreys, hawks, herons, and other unreleasable birds at this bird rehabilitation center. The birds live in spacious screened enclosures along a boardwalk running through some of the best waterfront real estate in the Keys. Rehabilitated birds are set free, whereas these have become permanent residents. Free birds—especially pelicans and egrets—come to visit. The center is popular among photographers, who arrive at 3:30 PM, when hundreds of wild waterbirds fly in and feed within arm's distance as the

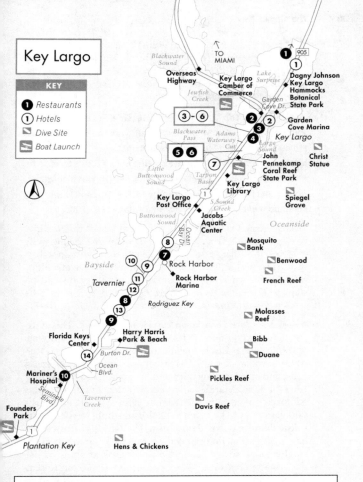

Key Largo

KEY
1 Restaurants
(1) Hotels
◣ Dive Site
⛴ Boat Launch

Blackwater
Sound

TO
MIAMI

Overseas
Highway

Jewfish
Creek

Key Largo
Camber of
Commerce

Lake
Surprise

905

Dagny Johnson
Key Largo
Hammocks
Botanical
State Park

Garden
Cove Dr.

Garden
Cove Marina

Key Largo

Blackwater
Pass

Adams
Waterway
Cut

Large
Sound

John
Pennekamp
Coral Reef
State Park

Christ
Statue

Little
Buttonwood
Sound

Tarpon
Basin

Key Largo
Library

Spiegel
Grove

Key Largo
Post Office

S.Sound
Creek

Oceanside

Buttonwood
Sound

Jacobs
Aquatic
Center

Bayside

Ocean Bay Dr.

Rock Harbor

Rock Harbor
Marina

Mosquito
Bank

Benwood

French Reef

Tavernier

Rodriguez Key

Molasses
Reef

Florida Keys
Center

Harry Harris
Park & Beach

Burton Dr.

Bibb

Duane

Mariner's
Hospital

Ocean
Blvd.

Pickles Reef

Founders
Park

Seminole Blvd.

Tavernier
Creek

Davis Reef

Plantation Key

Hens & Chickens

Restaurants
Alabama Jack's, **1**
Ballyhoo's, **7**
Chad's Deli & Bakery, **10**
The Fish House, **5**
The Fish House Encore, **4**
Harriette's Restaurant, **8**
Mrs. Mac's Kitchen, **2**
Rib Daddy's Steak &
Seafood, **6**
Snapper's, **9**
Sundowners, **3**

Hotels
Amy Slate's Amoray
Dive Resort, **3**
Azul Del Mar, **4**
Coconut Bay Resort & Bay
Harbor Lodge, **10**
Coconut Palm Inn, **14**
Dove Creek Lodge, **13**
John Pennekamp
Coral Reef State Park
Campground, **7**
Key Largo Grande Resort &
Beach Club, **1**

Kings Campground, **2**
Kona Kai Resort, **11**
Largo Lodge, **6**
Marriott's Key
Largo Bay
Beach Resort, **5**
The Pelican, **8**
Popp's Motel, **12**
Seafarer Resort, **9**

staff tries to draw in injured animals. A short nature trail runs into the mangrove forest (bring bug spray May to October). ⌂ *93600 Overseas Hwy. (MM 93.6, BS), Tavernier* ☎ *305/852–4486* ⊕ *www.fkwbc.org* 🖙 *Free, donations accepted* ⊙ *Daily sunrise–sunset.*

MAKING MOVIES. The 1948 film noir classic *Key Largo*, starring Humphrey Bogart and Lauren Bacall, was the most famous movie filmed in the Florida Keys, but not the only one. Others have included *Beneath the Twelve Mile Reef, PT 109, License to Kill, True Lies, Speed 2,* and *Red Dragon*. Key Largo is also where Bogart and Katherine Hepburn filmed *The African Queen*. The steamboat used in the movie is on display at MM 100.

🅒 **Jacobs Aquatic Center.** Take the plunge at one of three swimming pools: an 8-lane, 25-meter lap pool with a diving well; a 3- to 4-foot-deep pool accessible to people with mobility problems; and an interactive play pool with a waterslide, pirate ship, waterfall, and sloping zero entry instead of steps. ⌂ *320 Laguana Ave. (MM 99.6 OS)* ☎ *305/453–7946* ⊕ *www.jacobsaquaticcenter.org* 🖙 *$8–$10* ⊙ *Daily 10–7.*

★ Fodor'sChoice **John Pennekamp Coral Reef State Park.** This state
🅒 park is on everyone's list for close access to the best diving and snorkeling sites in the Sunshine State. The underwater treasure encompasses 78 square mi of coral reefs, sea-grass beds, and mangrove swamps and lies adjacent to the Florida Keys National Marine Sanctuary, which contains 40 of the 52 species of coral in the Atlantic Reef System and nearly 600 varieties of fish, from the colorful stoplight parrot fish to the demure cocoa damselfish. The park's visitor center has a 30-gallon floor-to-ceiling fish tank surrounded by smaller ones, so you can get a closer look at many of the underwater creatures. When you want to head out to sea, a concessionaire rents kayaks and powerboats, as well as snorkeling and diving equipment. You can also sign up for snorkeling and diving trips ($30 and $60, respectively) and glass-bottom-boat rides to the reef ($24). One of the most popular excursions is the snorkeling trip to see *Christ of the Deep,* the 2-ton underwater statue of Jesus. The park also has short nature trails, two man-made beaches, picnic shelters, a snack bar, and a campground. ⌂ *102601 Overseas Hwy. (MM 102.5 OS)* ☎ *305/451–1202 for park, 305/451–6300 for excursions* ⊕ *www.pennekamppark.com* 🖙 *$4.50 for 1 person, $9 for 2 people, 50¢ each additional person* ⊙ *Daily 8–sunset.*

2

Overseas Highway. From the mainland, taking this route, rather than Card Sound Road, lands you closer to Key Largo proper, abounding with shopping centers, chain restaurants, and, of course, dive shops.

WHERE TO EAT

$ ✕**Alabama Jack's.** *Seafood.* Calories be damned—the mammoth conch fritters here are heaven on a plate. The crab cakes, made from local blue crabs, earn hallelujahs, too. The conch salad is as good as any you'll find in the Bahamas and a third of the price in trendy Keys restaurants. This weathered, circa-1950 restaurant floats on two roadside barges in an old fishing community. Regulars include weekend cyclists, Miamians on the lam, and boaters, who come to admire tropical birds in the nearby mangroves, the occasional crocodile or manatee in the canal, or the bands that play on weekend afternoons until closing. ■TIP➔ **It's about a half-hour drive from Key Largo, so you may want to plan a visit for your drive in or out.** Jack's closes by 7, when the mosquitoes start biting. ⊠ *58000 Card Sound Rd. (just beyond the toll booth)* ☎ *305/248–8741* ⊕ *www.alabamajacks.com* ⊟ *MC, V.*

$$$ ✕**Ballyhoo's.** *Seafood.* Occupying a historic Conch house with an outdoor patio, this place is all about the fish (including the nicely nautical fish-house decor). Yellowtail snapper, one of the moistest, most flavorful local fish, is served eight different ways on the all-day menu, including blackened, stuffed with crab, and Parmesan-crusted. During stone-crab season (mid-October to mid-May), get in on the all-you-can-eat special. Typically Keys, the service is uneven at best, but the black beans and rice and the burgers settle the score. ⊠ *97800 Overseas Hwy. (MM 97.8 median)* ☎ *305/852–0822* ⊕ *www.ballyhoosrestaurant.com* ⊟ *AE, D, MC, V.*

$ ✕**Chad's Deli & Bakery.** *American.* It's a deli! It's a bakery! It's a pasta place! By day, Chad's serves monster sandwiches in pita wraps, rolls, or subs. After 2 PM it also offers pizza (try the garlic chicken white pizza) and pasta dishes. There's a good selection of beer and wine to wash it all down. Of course, you may bypass all this and make a meal out of one of Chad's seven varieties of cookies, approximately the size of your head, including white-chocolate macadamia-nut and chocolate-chip. ⊠ *92330 Overseas Hwy. (MM 92.3 BS)* ☎ *305/853–5566* ⊟ *MC, V.*

$$$ ×**The Fish House.** *Seafood.* Restaurants not on the water
★ have to produce the highest-quality food to survive in the
Keys. That's how the Fish House has succeeded since the
1980s—so much so that it built The Fish House Encore
next door to accommodate fans. The pan-sautéed grouper
will make you moan with pleasure, but it's just one of many
headliners in this nautical eatery. On the fin side, the choices
also include mahimahi, and yellowtail snapper that can be
broiled, blackened, jerked, or fried. The Matecumbe Catch
is the day's fresh fish prepared with tomatoes, capers, olive
oil, and lemon juice. Prefer shellfish? Choose from shrimp,
lobster, and (mid-October to mid-May) stone crab. For a
sweet ending, try the homemade key lime pie. ⊠ *102401
Overseas Hwy. (MM 102.4 OS)* ☎ *305/451–4665* ⊕ *www.
fishhouse.com* ⊟ *AE, D, MC, V* ⊙ *Closed Sept.*

$$$ ×**The Fish House Encore.** *Seafood.* To accommodate the crowds
that gather at the Fish House, the owners opened this place
with similar but more refined cuisine ranging from sushi to
steak. It has come into its own as a slightly more formal dining venue than its sister establishment. In the off-season you
can get your money's worth with $20 all-you-can-eat specials
such as mahimahi, snow crab, and peel 'n' eat shrimp. The
favorite, more casual place to dine is on the patio near the
trickling fountain. Live piano music entertains Thursday
through Sunday. ⊠ *102341 Overseas Hwy. (MM 102.3 OS)*
☎ *305/451–4665 or 305/451–0650* ⊕ *www.fishhouse.com*
⊟ *AE, D, MC, V* ⊙ *No lunch. Closed Oct.*

¢ ×**Harriette's Restaurant.** *American.* If you're looking for comfort food—like melt-in-your-mouth buttermilk biscuits—try
this 6 AM early bird. The kitchen makes fresh muffins daily,
in flavors like mango, chocolate, and key lime. Little has
changed over the years in this yellow-and-turquoise eatery.
Owner Harriette Mattson often personally greets guests
who come for steak and eggs with hash browns or old-
fashioned hotcakes with sausage or bacon. Stick to simple
dishes; the eggs Benedict is a disappointment. At lunch and
dinner time Harriette's shines in the burger department, but
there are also daily hot-meal specials such as chicken-fried
steak and turkey. ⊠ *95710 Overseas Hwy. (MM 95.7 BS)*
☎ *305/852–8689* ⊟ *MC, V* ⊙ *No dinner Fri.–Sun.*

$ ×**Mrs. Mac's Kitchen.** *Seafood.* Townies pack the counters and
★ booths at this tiny eatery where license plates are stuck on
the walls and made into chandeliers. Got a hankering for
meatloaf or crab cakes? You'll find them here, along with
specials like grilled yellowfin tuna. Bring your appetite for
the all-you-can-eat fish specials on Tuesday and Thursday.

There's also champagne breakfast, an assortment of tasty burgers and sandwiches, its famous chili, and key lime freeze (somewhere between a shake and a float). Ask about the daily hogfish special du jour. ✉ *99336 Overseas Hwy. (MM 99.4 BS)* ☎ *305/451–3722* ⊕ *www.mrsmacskitchen. com* 🖃 *AE, D, MC, V* ☺ *Closed Sun.*

$$$ ✕ **Rib Daddy's Steak & Seafood.** *Seafood.* Two Key Largo
☽ sister operations combined to create a comfort-food haven open for breakfast, lunch, and dinner. Dieters, keep driving. Sunday's brunch buffet has everything the restaurant is famous for with a $14.95 price tag. You'll swoon after tasting the Memphis-style smoked prime rib, Kobe strip steak, and barbecue chicken flavored with specially formulated rubs and sauces. The menu includes seafood options, too, such as crab cakes and all-you-can-eat lobster and stone crab specials. Try the Hemingway (fried mahi, eggs, and grits) for breakfast or the hand-pulled pork sandwich and Frito-chili cheeseburger for lunch. Save room for the key lime pie, creamy mango pie, or coconut cake. Kids love staring at the reef aquarium, the highlight of this rather plain, open dining room. ✉ *102570 Overseas Hwy. (MM 102.2 BS)* ☎ *305/451–0900* ⊕ *www.ribdaddysrestaurant. com* ⌕ *Reservations not accepted* 🖃 *AE, D, MC, V.*

$$ ✕ **Snapper's.** *Seafood.* If you bring in your ready-for-the-
★ grill fish, dinner here is $12 for a single, $13.95 per person family style. Otherwise, they'll catch and cook you a plank-roasted yellowtail snapper, grilled tuna steak, fish of the day baked with 36 herbs and spices, or a little something from the raw bar. The ceviche of yellowtail, shrimp, and conch (merrily spiced) wins raves, too. Not for the weak of heart is the Nutty Lobster appetizer, a spiny lobster covered with mixed nuts and thrown into the deep fryer. Slightly healthier, the key lime lobster is served over linguine. The seafood burrito is a keeper, plus there are a few Thai-inspired seafood preparations on the all-day menu. All of this is served up in a lively, mangrove-ringed waterfront setting with live music, an aquarium bar, Sunday brunch (including a Finlandia Bloody Mary bar), killer rum drinks, and seating alongside the boat dock. ✉ *139 Seaside Ave. (take Ocean View Blvd. off Hwy. 1) (MM 94.5 OS)* ☎ *305/852–5956* ⊕ *www.snapperskeylargo.com* 🖃 *AE, D, MC, V.*

$$$ ✕ **Sundowners.** *American.* The name doesn't lie. If it's a clear night and you can snag a reservation, this restaurant will treat you to a sherbet-hued sunset over Florida Bay. If you're here in mild weather—anytime other than the dog

days of summer or the rare winter cold snap—the best seats are on the patio. The food is excellent: try the key lime seafood, a happy combo of sautéed shrimp, lobster, and lump crabmeat swimming in a tangy sauce spiked with Tabasco served over penne or rice. Wednesday and Saturday are all about prime rib, and Friday draws the crowds with an all-you-can-eat fish fry ($16). Sunday brunch offers a changing selection of dishes and Bloody Marys. ⊠ *103900 Overseas Hwy. (MM 104 BS)* ☎ *305/451–4502* ⊕ *sundownerskeylargo.com* ⊟ *AE, D, MC, V.*

WHERE TO STAY

$$–$$$ ☖ **Amy Slate's Amoray Dive Resort.** The double entendre in its name sums up this hotel's dual charms. Read as "a moray," it refers to the moray eels you'll encounter on the reef. Read "amore," Italian for love, it calls to mind the place's romantic atmosphere. One- and two-story clapboard and stucco cottages huddle haphazardly around the property's marina and sandy beach. A five-star PADI-certified dive facility, it's a great place to rent equipment or take courses. Unlike many other resorts, Amoray offers single rooms. **Pros:** top-notch dive operation; free use of kayaks and snorkel equipment. **Cons:** noise from highway. ⊠ *104250 Overseas Hwy. (MM 104.2 BS)* ☎ *305/451–3595 or 800/426–6729* ⊕ *www.amoray.com* ⊅ *23 rooms, 8 apartments* ♿ *In-room: a/c, kitchen (some), refrigerator, Wi-Fi. In-hotel: pool, beachfront, diving, laundry facilities, Wi-Fi hotspot* ⊟ *AE, MC, V.*

$$$– ☖ **Azul del Mar.** The dock points the way to many beauti-
$$$$ ful sunsets at this adults-only boutique hotel. Advertis-
  ★   ing executive Karol Marsden and her husband, Dominic, a commercial travel photographer, transformed a run-down mom-and-pop place into this waterfront gem. As you'd expect from innkeepers with a background in the image business, the property offers great visuals, from marble floors and granite countertops to yellow-leather sofas and ice-blue bathroom tiles. Kayaks, barbecue grills, and a movie library are available for guest use, and two chickee huts on the beach are equipped with DVD players and comfortable seating. Wilderness kayaking and sunset bird-watching boat excursions explore what's best about the Keys. **Pros:** great garden; good location; sophisticated design. **Cons:** small beach; close to highway; high-priced. ⊠ *104300 Overseas Hwy. (MM 104.3 BS)* ☎ *305/451–0337 or 888/253–2985* ⊕ *www.azulhotels.us* ⊅ *2 studios, 3*

1-bedroom suites, 1 2-bedroom suite In-room: no phone, a/c, kitchen, DVD, Wi-Fi. In-hotel: beachfront, water sports, Wi-Fi hotspot, no kids under 16 ≡AE, D, MC, V.

$–$$ ▦ **Coconut Bay Resort & Bay Harbor Lodge.** Some 200 feet of waterfront is the main attraction at this property, a combination of two lodging options. Coconut palms whisper in the breeze, and gumbo-limbo trees shade the 2½-acre grounds. Nice features abound, like well-placed lounge chairs for gazing out over the water and kayaks and paddleboats (for when you want to get closer). Everybody shows up on the sundeck or the 16-foot dock to watch the sun slip into Davy Jones's Locker. Rooms are a bit tight, but not without island character. Pale-yellow cottages are simply furnished. Ask for Unit 25 and 26, a two-bedroom villa if you want extra space and a water view. **Pros:** bay front; neatly kept gardens; walking distance to restaurants; complimentary kayak and paddleboat use. **Cons:** a bit dated; small sea-walled sand beach. ✉ *97702 Overseas Hwy. (MM 97.7 BS)* ☎ *305/852–1625 or 800/385–0986* ⊕ *www.coconutbaykeylargo.com or www.bayharborkeylargo.com* ⇨ *7 rooms, 5 efficiencies, 2 suites, 1 2-bedroom villa, 6 1-bedroom cottages* & *In-room: a/c, kitchen (some), refrigerator, Wi-Fi (some). In-hotel: pool, beachfront, Wi-Fi hotspot, some pets allowed* ≡*AE, D, MC, V.*

$$$ ▦ **Coconut Palm Inn.** This low-key inn is set in a quiet residential neighborhood of towering gumbo-limbo and buttonwood trees. Built in the 1930s, the waterfront lodge draws repeat guests with its friendly, relaxed vibe. A 400-foot sandy beach is dotted with the requisite hammocks and swaying palm trees. Screened porches are a welcome touch, letting tropical breezes in and keeping mosquitoes out. Well-appointed accommodations are decorated in a tropical style, and range from standard rooms to one- and two-bedroom suites. No two are alike, although sea-foam-green paint is used liberally. A boccie-ball court and sunset yoga classes provide diversion. **Pros:** lovely beach; tranquil location; complimentary use of kayaks and paddleboats. **Cons:** off the beaten path. ✉ *198 Harborview Dr. (take Jo-Jean Way off Overseas Hwy.) (MM 92 BS), Tavernier* ☎ *305/852–3017* ⊕ *www.coconutpalminn.com* ⇨ *10 rooms, 7 suites* & *In-room: no phone, a/c, kitchen (some), refrigerator, Wi-Fi. In-hotel: pool, beachfront, laundry facilities, Wi-Fi hotspot, some pets allowed* ≡ *MC, V* ⊚*CP.*

$$$$ ▦ **Dove Creek Lodge.** Old-school anglers will likely be scandalized by this 2004 fishing camp's sherbet-hued paint and plantation-style furnishings. But when they get a load of the massive flat-screen TV, the comfy leather couch, and the stack of fishing magazines in the lobby, they might never want to leave. You can head out on a boat from the marina, chase billfish offshore or bonefish on the flats, and come to brag to your buddies about the one that got away. The surprisingly plush rooms range in size from simple lodge rooms to luxury suites, all with private screened porch or balcony. Avoid rooms 201 and 202 to get away from the "lively" noise from the seafood restaurant next door. **Pros:** great for fishing enthusiasts; luxurious rooms; close to Snapper's restaurant. **Cons:** loud music next door. ⊠ *147 Seaside Ave. (take Ocean View Blvd. off Hwy. 1) (MM 94.5 OS)* ☎ *305/852–6200 or 800/401–0057* ⊕ *www. dovecreeklodge.com* ➫ *4 rooms, 10 suites* ⚂ *In-room: a/c, safe, kitchen (some), refrigerator, Wi-Fi. In-hotel: pool, Wi-Fi hotspot* ⊟ *AE, D, MC, V* ⦿ *CP.*

$$$–
$$$$ 🖵 **Key Largo Grande Resort & Beach Club.** Nestled within a hardwood hammock (localese for uplands habitat where hardwood trees such as live oak grow) near the southern border of Everglades National Park, this sprawling hotel got a $12 million makeover in 2008. Spacious guest rooms each have a private balcony; most rooms overlook the water or woods, but some face the parking lot. Nature trails and boardwalks lead through the old-growth woods to a small, neatly groomed beach. Two small pools are separated by a coral-rock wall and two-sided waterfall. TreeTops Bar & Grill has great views, but service is slow. **Pros:** nice nature trail on bay side; pretty pools with waterfalls; awesome trees. **Cons:** pools near the highway; $12 per night for parking. ⊠ *97000 Overseas Hwy. (MM 97 BS)* ☎ *305/852– 5553 or 888/871–3437* ⊕ *www.keylargogrande.com* ➫ *190 rooms, 10 suites* ⚂ *In-room: a/c, safe, refrigerator (some). In-hotel: 2 restaurants, room service, bars, tennis courts, pools, gym, beachfront, water sports, bicycles, some pets allowed* ⊟ *AE, D, DC, MC, V.*

★ **Fodor's**Choice **Kona Kai Resort & Gallery.** Brilliantly colored
$$$$ bougainvilleas, coconut palms, guava trees, and a botanical garden make this 2-acre hideaway one of the prettiest places to stay in the Keys. Each of the intimate cottages has creative furnishings that add to the tropical feel. Spacious studios and one- and two-bedroom suites—with full kitchens and original art—are filled with natural light. Outside, kick back in a lounge chair or hammock on the beach, soak in the hot tub, or contemplate sunset from the deck. The resort also has an art gallery and an orchid house with more than 225 plants. Maid service is every third day to prolong

your privacy; however, fresh linens and towels are available at any time. At the pool, help yourself to complimentary bottled water and fruit. **Pros:** lush landscaping; free use of sports equipment; knowledgeable staff. **Cons:** expensive rates; some rooms are very close together. ✉ *97802 Overseas Hwy. (MM 97.8 BS)* ☎ *305/852-7200 or 800/365-7829* ⊕ *www.konakairesort.com* ⤵ *8 suites, 3 rooms* ⚠ *In-room: no phone, a/c, kitchen (some), refrigerator, DVD. In-hotel: tennis court, pool, beachfront, Wi-Fi hotspot, no kids under 16* ▭ *AE, D, MC, V* ⊙ *Closed Sept.*

$$$ ▦ **Largo Lodge.** When you drive under the dense canopy of
★ foliage at the entrance to Largo Lodge you'll feel like you've escaped Highway 1's bustle. Vintage 1950s cottages are tucked amid 3 acres of palm trees, sea grapes, and orchids. Cottage accommodations—surprisingly spacious—feature small kitchen and dining areas and large screened porches. Two bayfront rooms have been newly renovated, and the cottages too are benefitting from a recent change in ownership. A lavish swath of bay frontage is perfect for communing with the friendly squirrels, iguanas, and ibises. For swimming, you'll need to drive about 1 mi to John Pennekamp Coral Reef State Park, but kayak use is complimentary here. **Pros:** lush grounds; great sunset views; affordable rates; boat docking. **Cons:** no pool; some traffic noise outdoors. ✉ *101740 Overseas Hwy. (MM 101.7 BS)* ☎ *305/451-0424 or 800/468-4378* ⊕ *www.largolodge.com* ⤵ *2 rooms, 6 cottages* ⚠ *In-room: no phone, a/c, kitchen (some), refrigerator, Wi-Fi. In-hotel: beachfront, Wi-Fi hotspot, no kids under 14* ▭ *MC, V.*

$$$$ ▦ **Marriott's Key Largo Bay Beach Resort.** Park the car and toss
★ the keys in the bottom of your bag; there's no need to go
☼ anywhere else (except maybe John Pennekamp Coral Reef State Park, just a half mile north). This 17-acre bayside resort has plenty of diversions, from diving to parasailing to a day spa. Given all that, the pool still rules, so a stroll to the tiki bar could well be your most vigorous activity of the day. The resort's lemon-yellow facade exudes an air of warm, indolent days. This isn't the poshest chain hotel you've ever encountered, but it's fresh-looking and suitably tropical in style. Some of the best rooms and suites offer sunset views. **Pros:** lots of activities; free covered parking; lovely pool; free Wi-Fi. **Cons:** rooms facing highway can be noisy; thin walls; unspectacular beach. ✉ *103800 Overseas Hwy. (MM 103.8 BS)* ☎ *305/453-0000 or 866/849-3753* ⊕ *www.marriottkeylargo.com* ⤵ *132 rooms, 20 2-bedroom suites, 1 penthouse suite* ⚠ *In-room: a/c, safe, kitchen*

(some), Wi-Fi. In-hotel: 3 restaurants, room service, bars, pool, gym, spa, beachfront, diving, water sports, bicycles, children's programs (ages 5–13), laundry facilities, laundry service, Wi-Fi hotspot, some pets allowed ▭ *AE, D, DC, MC, V.*

¢–$ **The Pelican.** This 1950s throwback is reminiscent of the days when parents packed the kids into the station wagon and headed to no-frills seaside motels, complete with fishing off the dock. The owners have spiffed things up with cute, artsy touches and added a small sunning beach, but basically it's just a motel, not fancy but comfortable. Guests here don't mind skimping on space and a few frills in favor of homey digs, socializing under the chickee, and a low price tag. **Pros:** free use of kayaks and paddleboats; well-maintained dock; reasonable rates. **Cons:** some small rooms; basic accommodations and amenities. ✉ *99340 Overseas Hwy. (MM 99.3 BS)* ☎ *305/451–3576 or 877/451–3576* 🌐 *www.thepelicankeylargo.com* ⇨ *13 rooms, 4 efficiencies, 4 suites* *In-room: no phone, a/c, kitchen (some), refrigerator, DVD, Wi-Fi. In-hotel: beachfront, water sports, laundry facilities, Wi-Fi hotspot* ▭ *AE, D, DC, MC, V* 🍽 *CP.*

$$$ **Popp's Motel.** Stylized metal herons mark the entrance to this 50-year-old family-run motel. The third and fourth generations of the Popp family are currently at the helm, taking care of the basic-but-clean units. Don't be discouraged by the building clutter around the office. Inside the rooms bright paint jobs, shiny terrazzo floors, and modern kitchens contrast. Room 9 is closest to the beach. Family-friendly as it seems, no kids under age 13 are welcome. **Pros:** nice beach; intimate feel. **Cons:** limited amenities; two-night minimum stay required. ✉ *95500 Overseas Hwy. (MM 95.5 BS)* ☎ *305/852–5201 or 877/852–5210* 🌐 *www.popps.com* ⇨ *9 units* *In-room: a/c, kitchen. In-hotel: beachfront, no kids under age 13* ▭ *AE, MC, V.*

¢–$ **Seafarer Resort.** It's budget lodging, but the Seafarer Resort is not without its charms. There's a pond and hammocks, most rooms have water views, and some have private patios. Rooms 3 and 4 are spacious and best for families. Unit 6, a one-bedroom cottage called the Beach House, has a large picture window with an awesome view of the bay. Guests gather at the beachfront picnic table for alfresco dining and on the dock and lounge chairs for sunset-watching. **Pros:** sandy beach; complimentary kayak use. **Cons:** some rooms close to road noise; basic accommodations. ✉ *97684 Overseas Hwy. (MM 97.6 BS)* ☎ *305/852–5349* 🌐 *www.seafarerresort.com* ⇨ *8 rooms,*

3 studios, 3 1-bedroom cottages, 1 2-bedroom cottage, 2 apartments ₺In-room: no phone, a/c, kitchen (some), refrigerator. In-hotel: beachfront, water sports, laundry facilities, Wi-Fi hotspot ⊟MC, V.

CAMPGROUNDS

★ ⚠ **John Pennekamp Coral Reef State Park**. Divers and snorkel-
☺ ers won't find a better location in the Upper Keys. Pen-
nekamp's campsites are carved out of hardwood hammock, providing shade and privacy away from the heavy day-use areas. Activities include boating, fishing, scuba diving, snorkeling, and hiking. There's no restaurant, but there are vending machines for late-night snack attacks. *₺Flush toilets, partial hookups (electric and water), dump station, drinking water, showers, fire pits, picnic tables, electricity, public telephone, general store, ranger station, swimming (ocean) ⟿47 partial hookups for RVs and tents ✉102601 Overseas Hwy. (MM 102.5 OS) ☎305/451–1202 park, 800/326–3521 reservations ⊕www.reserveamerica.com ⊟AE, D, MC, V.*

⚠ **Kings Kamp**. Florida Bay breezes keep things cool at this campground, and the neighboring waterway gives boaters direct access to John Pennekamp Coral Reef State Park. The campground has a marina for storing boats ($10 per day). The park can accommodate RVs up to 40 feet long, and if you don't want to bring your own, you can rent one ($110–$125). This property also has a cottage ($125–$150), motel-style units ($55–$85), and tent sites ($40–$50). *₺Partial hookups (electric and water), dump station, drinking water, picnic tables, electricity, public telephone, swimming (ocean), Wi-Fi hotspot ⟿60 hookups for RVs and tents ✉103620 Overseas Hwy. (MM 103.5 BS) ☎305/451–0010 ⊕www.kingskamp.com ⊟MC, V.*

NIGHTLIFE

The semiweekly *Keynoter* (Wednesday and Saturday), weekly *Reporter* (Thursday), and Friday through Sunday editions of the *Miami Herald* are the best sources of information on entertainment and nightlife. Daiquiri bars, tiki huts, and seaside shacks pretty well summarize Key Largo's bar scene.

Mingle with resort guests and locals over cocktails and sunsets at elevated **Breezers Tiki Bar & Grille** (✉*103800 Overseas Hwy. [MM 103.8 BS]* ☎*305/453–0000*), in Marriott's Key Largo Bay Beach Resort. Walls plastered with Bogart memorabilia remind customers that the classic 1948 Bogart-Bacall flick *Key Largo* has a connection with the **Caribbean Club** (✉ *MM 104 BS* ☎ *305/451–4466*). It draws boaters, curious visitors, and local barfly types, happiest while they're shooting the breeze or shooting pool. Postcard-perfect sunsets and live music draw revelers on weekends.

Coconuts (✉ *Marina Del Mar Resort, 528 Caribbean Dr. [MM 100 OS]* ☎ *305/453–9794*) has live music indoors and outdoors throughout most of the week. Outside around the resort pool it's a family scene, with food service and a bar. Inside is strictly a thirty- and forty-something crowd, sprinkled with a few more-seasoned townies playing pool, watching sports TV, and enjoying the music.

SPORTS AND THE OUTDOORS

BIKING

Not as big a pursuit as on other islands, biking can be a little dangerous along Key Largo's main drag. Parts of the still-developing Florida Keys Overseas Heritage Trail take you off Highway 1 along Old Highway.

Bubba's (☎ *321/759–3433* ⊕ *www.bubbafestbiketours.com*) organizes custom biking tours through the Keys along the heritage trail. A van accompanies tours to carry luggage and tired riders. Operated by former police officer Bubba Barron, Bubba's hosts an annual one-week ride down the length of the Keys every November. Riders can opt for tent camping ($595) or motel-room accommodations. Meals are included and bike rentals are extra.

BOATING

Captain Sterling's **Everglades Eco-Tours** (✉ *Dolphin's Cove [MM 102 BS], Key Largo* ☎ *305/853–5161 or 888/224–6044* ⊕ *www.captainsterling.com*) operates Everglades and Florida Bay ecology tours ($50 per person) and sunset cruises ($75 per person).

Key Largo Princess (✉ *99701 Overseas Hwy. [MM 100 OS], Key Largo* ☎ *305/451–4655 or 877/648–8129* ⊕ *www.keylargoprincess.com*) offers two-hour glass-bottom-boat trips ($30) and sunset cruises on a luxury 70-foot motor yacht with a 280-square-foot glass viewing area, departing from the Holiday Inn docks three times a day.

CANOEING AND KAYAKING

Sea kayaking continues to gain popularity in the Keys. You can paddle for a few hours or the whole day, on your own or with a guide. Some outfitters even offer overnight trips. The **Florida Keys Overseas Paddling Trail**, part of a statewide system, runs from Key Largo to Key West. You can paddle the entire distance, 110 mi on the Atlantic side, which takes 9–10 days. The trail also runs the chain's length on the bay side, which is a longer route.

At John Pennekamp Coral Reef State Park, **Coral Reef Park Co.** (⊠ *102601 Overseas Hwy. [MM 102.5 OS]* ☎ *305/451–6300* ⊕ *www.pennekamppark.com*) has a fleet of canoes and kayaks for gliding around the 2½-mi mangrove trail or along the coast. It also rents powerboats.

Rent canoes or sea kayaks or standup paddleboards from **Florida Bay Outfitters** (⊠ *104050 Overseas Hwy. [MM 104 BS]* ☎ *305/451–3018* ⊕ *www.kayakfloridakeys.com*). The company, which helps with trip planning and matches equipment to your skill level, sets up self-guided trips on the Florida Keys Overseas Paddling Trail. It also runs myriad guided tours around Key Largo. Take a full-moon paddle, or a one- to seven-day canoe or kayak tour to the Everglades, Lignumvitae Key, or Indian Key. Trips run $60–$795.

DOLPHIN INTERACTION PROGRAMS

The Keys have the greatest concentration of places where visitors can interact with dolphins. Some people, especially children, love learning about the dolphins and seeing them up close, while others bristle at seeing the animals kept in captivity to serve public whims. If you're among the latter, you'll want to avoid these programs and perhaps opt for a dolphin-spotting tour in the wild (but even these are questioned by some environmentalists if the tour operators do anything to attract the dolphins to the boat). Feeding them is strictly taboo, but some tour operators slap the side of the boat and circle around the spotted dolphin. For listings of businesses that are recognized as dolphin-friendly by the National Oceanic and Atmospheric Administration (NOAA), visit ⊕ *www.dolphinsmart.org*.

The educational program at **Dolphin Cove** (⊠ *101900 Overseas Hwy. [MM 101.9, BS], Key Largo* ☎ *305/451–4060 or 877/365–2683* ⊕ *www.dolphinscove.com*) begins at the facility's lagoon with a get-acquainted session from a platform. After that, you slip into the water for some frolick-

ing with your new dolphin pals. The cost is $125 to $185.
Spend the day shadowing a dolphin trainer for $630.

Dolphins Plus (✉ *31 Corrine Pl. [MM 99], Key Largo* ☎ *305/
451–1993 or 866/860–7946* ⊕ *www.dolphinsplus.com*)
programs emphasize education and conservation. Costing $135, the Natural Swim program begins with a one-
hour briefing; then you enter the water to become totally
immersed in the dolphins' world. No touching or interacting is allowed. For that, sign up for the $185 Structured
Swim program. A Sea Lion Swim costs $120.

FISHING
Private charters and big head boats (so named because they
charge "by the head") are great for anglers who don't have
their own vessel.

Sailors Choice (✉ *Holiday Inn Resort & Marina, 99701 Overseas Hwy. [MM 100 OS]* ☎ *305/451–1802 or 305/451–
0041* ⊕ *www.sailorschoicefishingboat.com*) has fishing
excursions departing twice daily ($40 for half-day trips).
The 65-foot boat leaves from the Holiday Inn docks. Rods,
bait, and license are included.

SCUBA DIVING AND SNORKELING
Much of what makes the Upper Keys a singular dive destination is variety. Places like Molasses Reef, which begins 3
feet below the surface and descends to 55 feet, have something for everyone from novice snorkelers to experienced
divers. The *Spiegel Grove*, a 510-foot vessel, lies in 130 feet
of water, but its upper regions are only 60 feet below the
surface. On rough days, Key Largo Undersea Park's Emerald Lagoon is a popular spot. Expect to pay about $80 for
a two-tank, two-site-dive trip with tanks and weights, or
$35–$40 for a two-site snorkel outing. Get big discounts
by booking multiple trips.

Amy Slate's Amoray Dive Resort (✉ *104250 Overseas Hwy.
[MM 104.2 BS]* ☎ *305/451–3595 or 800/426–6729* ⊕ *www.
amoray.com*) makes diving easy. Stroll down to the full-
service dive shop (NAUI, PADI, TDI, and BSAC certifica-
tions honored), then onto a 45-foot catamaran. The rate
for a two-dive trip is $80 including tanks and weights.

★ **Conch Republic Divers** (✉ *90800 Overseas Hwy. [MM 90.8
BS]* ☎ *305/852–1655 or 800/274–3483* ⊕ *www.conchre-
publicdivers.com*) offers instruction as well as scuba and
snorkeling tours of all the wrecks and reefs of the Upper
Keys. Two-location dives are $80 with tank and weights.

Coral Reef Park Co. (✉ *102601 Overseas Hwy. [MM 102.5 OS]* ☎ *305/451–6300* ⊕ *www.pennekamppark.com*), at John Pennekamp Coral Reef State Park, gives 3½-hour scuba ($60) and 2½-hour snorkeling ($30) tours of the park. Besides the great location and the dependability of this operation, it's suited for water adventurers of all levels.

Horizon Divers (✉ *100 Ocean Dr. #1, Key Largo* ☎ *305/453–3535 or 800/984–3483* ⊕ *www.horizondivers.com*) has customized diving (starting from $80), and snorkeling (starting from $50) trips that depart daily aboard a 45-foot catamaran.

Island Ventures (✉ *103900 Overseas Hwy. [MM 103.9] at Sundowner's Restaurant, Key Largo* ☎ *305/451–4957* ⊕ *www.islandventure.com*) provides daily excursions that take you snorkeling or scuba diving. Scuba trips, offered twice daily, are $80 including tanks and weights; snorkeling trips are $45 each. Ride-alongs pay $35.

Keys Diver Snorkel Tours (✉ *99696 Overseas Hwy. [MM 100 BS], Key Largo* ☎ *305/451–1177* ⊕ *www.keysdiver.com*) offers snorkel and dive trips that take you to Key Largo National Marine Sanctuary. Two-tank dives include a restaurant lunch for $80 each; snorkel excursions range $28.95 for one location to $35.95 for three.

Ocean Divers (✉ *522 Caribbean Dr. [MM 105.5 BS]* ✉ *105800 Overseas Hwy. [MM 100 OS]* ☎ *305/451–0037 or 800/451–1113* ⊕ *www.oceandivers.com*) operates two shops in Key Largo. The PADI five-star Caribbean Drive facility offers day and night dives, a range of courses, and dive-lodging packages. The cost is $80 for a two-tank reef dive with tank and weight rental. Snorkel trips from the other shop cost $5 with snorkel, mask, and fins provided.

Quiescence Diving Services (✉ *103680 Overseas Hwy. [MM 103.5 BS]* ☎ *305/451–2440* ⊕ *www.quiescence.com*) sets itself apart in two ways: it limits groups to six to ensure personal attention and offers day and night dives, as well as twilight dives when sea creatures are most active. Two-dive trips start at $66 without equipment.

SHOPPING

For the most part, shopping is sporadic in Key Largo, with a couple of shopping centers and fewer galleries than you find on the other big islands. If you're looking to buy scuba or snorkel equipment, you'll have plenty of places from which to choose.

Bluewater Potters (✉ *102991 Overseas Hwy. [MM 102.9 OS],* ☎ *305/453–1920* ⊕ *www.bluewaterpotters.com*) creates functional and decorative pieces ranging from signature vases and kitchenware to one-of-a-kind pieces where the owners' creative talent at the wheel blazes.

Pick up an old Hemingway novel or the latest tome from a local poet at **Cover to Cover Books** (✉ *Pelican Plaza, 86713 Overseas Hwy. [MM 86.7 BS]* ☎ *305/853–2464*). The children's department is especially interesting. There's also a coffee bar with Wi-Fi.

Original works by major international artists—including sea captain–turned-painter Dirk Verdoorn, Italian artist Franco Passalaqua, and French sculptor Polles—are shown at the **Gallery at Kona Kai** (✉ *97802 Overseas Hwy. [MM 97.8 BS]* ☎ *305/852–7200* ⊕ *www.g-k-k.com*), in the Kona Kai Resort.

Go into olfactory overload—you'll find yourself sniffing every single bar of soap and scented candle—at **Key Lime Products** (✉ *95200 Overseas Hwy. [MM 95.2 BS]* ☎ *305/853–0378 or 800/870–1780* ⊕ *keylimeproducts.com*). Take home some key lime juice and bake a pie; the super-easy directions are right on the bottle. Shop for everything from key lime marmalade to key lime shampoo.

You can find lots of shops in the Keys that sell cheesy souvenirs—snow globes, alligator hats, and shell-encrusted anything. **Shellworld** (✉ *97600 Overseas Hwy. [MM 97.5]* ☎ *305/852–8245* ⊕ *www.shellworldflkeys.com*) is the granddaddy of them all. This sprawling building in the median of the Overseas Highway has clothing, jewelry, and souvenirs from delightfully tacky to tasteful.

ISLAMORADA

Islamorada is between mile markers 90.5 and 70.

Early settlers named this key after their schooner, *Island Home,* but to make it sound more romantic they translated it into Spanish: *Isla Morada*. The chamber of commerce prefers to use its literal translation "Purple Island," which refers either to a purple-shelled snail that once inhabited these shores or to the brilliantly colored orchids and bougainvilleas.

2

Early maps show Islamorada as encompassing only Upper Matecumbe Key. But the incorporated "Village of Islands" is made up of a string of islands that the Overseas Highway crosses, including Plantation Key, Windley Key, Upper Matecumbe Key, Lower Matecumbe Key, Craig Key, and Fiesta Key. In addition, two state-park islands accessible only by boat—Indian Key and Lignumvitae Key—belong to the group.

Islamorada (locals pronounce it *"eye*-la-mor-*ah*-da") is one of the world's top fishing destinations. For nearly 100 years seasoned anglers have fished these clear, warm waters teeming with trophy-worthy fish. There are numerous options for those in search of the big ones, including chartering a boat with its own crew or heading out on a vessel rented from one of the plethora of marinas along this 20-mi stretch of the Overseas Highway. More than 150 backcountry guides and 400 offshore captains are at your service.

Islamorada is one of the more affluent resort areas of the Keys. Sophisticated resorts and restaurants meet the needs of those in search of luxury, but there's also plenty for those looking for something more casual and affordable. Art galleries and boutiques make Islamorada's shopping scene the best in the Upper Keys, but if you're shopping for groceries, head to Marathon or Key Largo.

GETTING HERE AND AROUND
Most visitors arrive in Islamorada by car. If you're flying in to Miami International Airport or Key West International Airport, you can easily rent a car (reserve in advance) to make the drive.

ESSENTIALS
Visitor Information Islamorada Chamber of Commerce (✉ *MM 83.2 BS, Upper Matecumbe Key, Islamorada* ☎ *305/664–4503 or 800/322–5397* ⊕ *www.islamoradachamber.com*).

EXPLORING

TOP ATTRACTIONS

History of Diving Museum. Adding to the region's reputation for world-class diving, this museum plunges into the history of man's thirst for undersea exploration. Among its 13 galleries of interactive and other interesting displays are a submarine and helmet from the film *20,000 Leagues Under the Sea*. Historic equipment, sunken treasures, and photographs are part of the extensive collection donated by a local couple. ✉ *82990 Overseas Hwy. (MM 83 BS), Upper Matecumbe Key* ☎ *305/664–9737* ⊕ *www.divingmuseum. org* 🖭 *$12* ⊙ *Daily 10–5.*

★ **Robbie's Marina.** Huge, prehistoric-looking denizens of the ⟳ not-so-deep, silver-sided tarpon congregate around the docks at Robbie's Marina on Lower Matecumbe Key. Children—and lots of adults—pay $4 to feed them sardines or $1 just to watch. Spend some time hanging out at this authentic Keys community, where you can grab a bite to eat, do a little open-air shopping, or charter a boat. ✉ *77522 Overseas Hwy. (MM 77.5 BS), Lower Matecumbe Key* ☎ *305/664–9814 or 877/664–8498* ⊕ *www.robbies.com* 🖭 *Dock access $1* ⊙ *Daily 8–5.*

⟳ **Theater of the Sea.** The second-oldest marine-mammal center in the world doesn't attempt to compete with more modern, more expensive parks. Even so, it's among the better attractions north of Key West, especially if you have kids in tow. Like the pricier parks, there are dolphin, sea lion, and stingray encounters ($175, including general admission), where you can get up close and personal with underwater creatures. These are popular, so reserve in advance. Ride a "bottomless" boat to see what's below the waves and take a guided tour of the marine-life exhibits. Entertaining educational shows highlight conservation issues. You can stop for lunch at the grill, shop in the boutique, or sunbathe at a lagoon-side beach. This easily could be an all-day attraction. ✉ *84721 Overseas Hwy. (MM 84.5 OS), Windley Key* ☎ *305/664–2431* ⊕ *www.theaterofthesea.com* 🖭 *$27* ⊙ *Daily 9:30–5 (last ticket sold at 3:30).*

WORTH NOTING

Anne's Beach. On Lower Matecumbe Key, this beach, named for a local environmental activist, is a popular village park whose "beach" (really a typical Keys-style sand flat) is best enjoyed at low tide. The nicest feature here is a ½-mi, elevated, wooden boardwalk that meanders through a

Islamorada

TO TAVERNIER & KEY LARGO

KEY

- **1** Restaurants
- (1) Hotels
- Dive Site
- Boat Launch

Plantation Key

Founders Park

1 Giant Lobster

Snake Creek

Windley Key

Windley Key Fossil Reef Geological State Park

Whale Harbor Bridge

2

(2) Theater of the Sea

(3)

Hens & Chickens

Crocker Reef

3 4

History of Diving Museum

5 - 8

(4)

Upper Matecumbe Key

(5)

Hammer Head

(6) (7) Islamorada Country Park

Beach Rd.

Cheeca Rocks

The Garden

Shell Key

Parker Dr.

Oceanside

Lignumvitae Key

Papa Joes' Marina

Bud N' Mary's Marina

The Eagle

Ligumvitae Key Botanical State Park

Alligator Reef

Robbie's Marina

9

Indian Key Historic State Park

Bayside

Indian Key

Lasarra Ln.
Sea Ln.
Ocean Ln.
Sand Cove
Costa Brava
Toll Gate Blvd.

Lower Matecumbe Key

8 Caloosaa Cove Marina

Anne's Beach

TO MARATHON

Restaurants

Green Turtle Inn, **5**
Hungry Tarpon, **9**
Island Grill, **2**
Kaiyo, **4**
Lorelei Restaurant and Cabana Bar, **3**
Marker 88, **1**
Morada Bay Beach Cafe, **7**
Pierre's, **6**
Uncle's Restaurant, **8**

Hotels

Casa Morada, **5**
Cheeca Lodge & Spa, **6**
Chesapeake Beach Resort, **3**
Drop Anchor Resort & Marina, **2**
The Islander Resort, **4**
The Moorings, **7**
Ragged Edge Resort, **1**
White Gate Court, **8**

natural wetland hammock. Covered picnic areas along
the way give you places to linger and enjoy the view. Restrooms are at the north end. Weekends are packed with
Miami day-trippers, as it's the only public beach until you
reach Marathon. ⊠ *MM 73.5 OS, Lower Matecumbe Key*
☎ *305/853–1685.*

Indian Key Historic State Park. Mystery surrounds 10-acre
Indian Key, on the ocean side of the Matecumbe islands.
Before it became one of the first European settlements
outside of Key West, it was inhabited by American Indians
for several thousand years. The islet served as a base for
19th-century shipwreck salvagers until an Indian attack
wiped out the settlement in 1840. Dr. Henry Perrine, a
noted botanist, was killed in the raid. Today his plants
grow in the town's ruins. Most people kayak or canoe here
from Indian Key Fill to explore the nature trails and the
town ruins or snorkel. Florida Keys Kayak has an office at
Robbie's Marina. There are no restrooms or picnic facilities on the island. ⊕ *Box 1052* ☎ *305/664–2540* ⊕ *www.
floridastateparks.org/indiankey* ≋ *Free* ☉ *Daily 8* AM–*5* PM.

Islamorada Founder's Park. This public park boasts a palm-
shaded beach, swimming pool, marina, skate park, tennis,
and plenty of other facilities. If you want to rent a boat
or learn to sail, businesses here can help you. If you're
staying in Islamorada, admission is free and you pay an
additional $3 to use the Olympic-size pool. Those stay-
ing elsewhere pay $8 to enter the park and $4 for the
pool. A spiffy amphitheater hosts concerts, plays, and
shows. ⊠ *87000 Overseas Hwy. (MM 87 BS), Plantation
Key* ☎ *305/853–1685.*

Lignumvitae Key Botanical State Park. On the National Register
of Historic Places, this 280-acre bay-side island is the site
of a virgin hardwood forest and the 1919 home of chemical
magnate William Matheson. His caretaker's cottage serves
as the park's visitor center. Access is by boat—your own,
a rented vessel, or a ferry operated by Robbie's Marina.
(Paddling here from Indian Key Fill, at MM 78.5, is a popular pastime.) The only way to do the trails is by a guided
ranger walk, offered Thursday through Monday for ferry
passengers on the 10 and 2 excursions. Wear long sleeves
and pants, and bring mosquito repellent. The Lignumvitae
Christmas Celebration is on the first weekend in December.
⊕ *Box 1052* ☎ *305/664–2540 park, 305/664–9814 ferry*
⊕ *www.floridastateparks.org/lignumvitaekey* ≋ *Free; ferry*

and tour $35 ⊙ *Park open Thurs.–Mon. 9–5; house tours
Fri.–Sun. 10 and 2.*

Plantation Key. Between 1885 and 1915, settlers earned
good livings growing pineapples here by using Bahamian
workers to plant and harvest their crops. The plantations
that gave the place its name are long gone, replaced by a
dense concentration of homes, businesses, and a public
park. ⊠ *MM 90.5–86.*

Upper Matecumbe Key. One of the first of the Upper Keys
to be permanently settled, its early homesteaders were so
successful at growing pineapples in the rocky soil that at
one time the island yielded the country's largest annual
crop. However, foreign competition and the hurricane of
1935 killed the industry. Today life centers on fishing and
tourism, and the island is filled with bait shops, marinas,
and charter-fishing boats. ⊠ *MM 84–79.*

Windley Key. This is one of the highest points in the Keys,
though at 16 feet above sea level it's not likely to give anyone altitude sickness. Originally two islets, this area was
first inhabited by American Indians, who left behind a few
traces of their dwellings, and then by farmers and fishermen
who built their homes here in the mid-1800s. Henry Flagler
bought the land from homesteaders in 1908 for his Florida
East Coast Railway, filling in the inlet between what were
then called the Umbrella Keys. His workers quarried coral
rock for the rail bed and bridge approaches—the same rock
used in many historic South Florida structures, including
Miami's Vizcaya and the Hurricane Monument on Upper
Matecumbe. Although the Quarry Station was destroyed by
the 1935 hurricane, quarrying continued until the 1960s.
Today, there's little really to see here; the island consists
of a few resorts and a state park, but it's a good spot for
a walk. ⊠ *MM 86–84.*

Windley Key Fossil Reef Geological State Park. A fossilized
coral reef dating back about 125,000 years shows that the
Florida Keys were once beneath the ocean. Excavation of
Windley Key's limestone bed by the Florida East Coast Railway exposed the petrified reef, full of beautifully fossilized
brain coral and sea ferns. Visitors can see the fossils along
a 300-foot quarry wall when hiking the park's three trails.
There are guided (Friday, Saturday, and Sunday only) and
self-guided tours along the trails, which lead to the railway's old quarrying equipment and cutting pits, where you
can make rubbings of the quarry walls. The **Alison Fahrer**

Environmental Education Center holds historic, biological, and geological displays about the area, including videos. The first Saturday in March is Windley Key Day, when the park sells native plants and hosts environmental exhibits. ⊠*MM 84.9 BS, Windley Key* ☎*305/664–2540* ⊕*www. floridastateparks.org/windleykey* ⊠*Education center free, $2 for park self-tours, $1 for ranger-guided tours* ☉*Park Thurs.–Mon. 9–5; education center and tours Fri.–Sun. (tours at 10 and 2).*

WHERE TO EAT

$$$ ✕**Green Turtle Inn.** *Seafood.* This circa-1928 landmark inn and its vintage neon sign are a slice of Florida Keys history. Period photographs decorate the wood-paneled walls. Diners can feast on breakfast and lunch options like coconut French toast and yellowtail po'boy. Chef Dan Harris relies heavily on his homeland Cajun cuisine tossed with a Latin touches for the dinner menu; think turtle chowder (don't gasp; it's made from farm-raised freshwater turtles), churrasco steak with yucca hash, and crawfish étouffée. Naturally, there's a Turtle Sundae on the dessert menu. ⊠*81219 Overseas Hwy. (MM 81.2 OS), Upper Matecumbe Key* ☎*305/664–2006* ⊕*www.greenturtlekeys.com* ⊠*Reservations essential* ⊟*AE, MC, V* ☉*Closed Mon.*

$$$ ✕**Hungry Tarpon.** *Seafood.* As part of the colorful, bustling Old Florida scene at Robbie's Marina, you know that the seafood here is fresh and top-quality. The extensive menu seems as if it's bigger than the dining space, which consists of a few tables and some counter seating indoors, plus a smattering of tables out back, close to where tourists pay dollars to feed the tarpon in the marina. While tarpon are snacking on sardines, diners enjoy such breakfast, lunch, and dinner specialties as stacked crepes with fried eggs and lobster, huevos rancheros, grilled ahi tuna sandwich, shrimp burrito, lobster thermidor, and fish with brandy lobster cream sauce. ⊠*77522 Overseas Hwy. (MM 77.5 BS), Lower Matecumbe Key* ☎*305/664–0535* ⊕*www.hungrytarpon.com.*

$$ ✕**Island Grill.** *Seafood.* Don't be fooled by appearances; ★ this shack on the waterfront takes island breakfast, lunch, and dinner cuisine up a notch. The eclectic menu tempts you with dishes such as guava-barbecue shrimp wrapped in bacon, and lobster rolls. Southern-style shrimp and andouille sausage with grits join island-style specialties such as crispy whole yellowtail snapper on the list of entrées.

There's an air-conditioned dining room and bar as well as outdoor seating under the trees. The outdoor bar hosts live entertainment Wednesday to Sunday. ✉ *85501 Overseas Hwy. (MM 85.5 OS), Windley Key* ☎ *305/664–8400* ⊕ *www.keysislandgrill.com* ☰ *AE, D, MC, V.*

$$ ✕**Kaiyó.** *Japanese.* Kaiyó's decor—an inviting setting that
★ includes colorful abstract mosaics, polished wood floors, and upholstered banquettes—almost steals the show here, but the food is equally interesting. The menu, a fusion of East and West, offers sushi and sashimi and rolls that combine local ingredients with traditional Japanese tastes. The key lime lobster roll is a blend of tempura Florida lobster with hearts of palm and essence of key lime. The baby conch roll surrounds tempura conch, ponzu mayo, and kimchi with sushi rice for an inside-out effect. Entrées in the $22-and-up range include crab-stuffed soft-shell crab, teriyaki chicken, and macadamia-crusted yellowtail snapper with mango sauce. The Express Lunch Buffet spreads 30-some dishes for a $12.95 all-you-can-eat charge. ✉ *81701 Overseas Hwy. (MM 81.5 OS), Upper Matecumbe Key* ☎ *305/664–5556* ⊕ *www.kaiyokeys.com* ☰ *AE, MC, V* ⊙ *Closed Sun.*

$$ ✕**Lorelei Restaurant & Cabana Bar.** *American.* Local anglers gather here for breakfast. Lunch and dinner bring a mix of islanders and visitors for straightforward food and good times. Live bands ensure a lively nighttime scene, and the menu staves off inebriation with burgers, barbecued baby back ribs, and Parmesan-crusted snapper. Key lime pie comes frozen with mango sauce. ✉ *81924 Overseas Hwy. (MM 82 BS), Upper Matecumbe Key* ☎ *305/664–2692* ⊕ *www.loreleifloridakeys.com* ☰ *AE, MC, V.*

$$$ ✕**Marker 88.** *Seafood.* Located a few yards from Florida Bay,
★ this seafood restaurant has been popular for more than 40 years. Large picture windows offer great sunset views, but the bay is lovely no matter what time of day you visit. Chef Sal Barrios serves such irresistible entrées as onion-crusted mahi, crispy yellowtail snapper, and mangrove honey and chipotle–glazed rib eye. In addition, there are a half-dozen burgers and sandwiches, and you can't miss the restaurant's famous key lime baked Alaska dessert. The extensive wine list is a oenophile's delight. ✉ *88000 Overseas Hwy. (MM 88 BS), Plantation Key* ☎ *305/852–9315* ⊕ *www.marker88. info* ♨ *Reservations essential* ☰ *AE, D, MC, V.*

$$$ ✕**Morada Bay Beach Café.** *Eclectic.* This bay-front restau-
★ rant wins high marks for its surprisingly stellar cuisine,
☾ tables planted in the sand, and tiki torches that bathe the

evening in romance. Entrées feature alluring combinations like banana curry lobster, and wahoo (a meaty local fish) with carrot-ginger puree. Seafood takes center stage, but you can always get roasted organic chicken breast (stuffed with boursin and spinach) or a Wagyu burger. A tapas menu caters to smaller appetites: grouper ceviche, conch fritters, tuna rolls, and the like. Lunch adds interesting sandwiches to the mix. Sit in a dining room outfitted with surfboards, or outdoors on a beach, where the sunset puts on a mighty show and kids (and your feet) play in the sand. There's nightly live music and a monthly full-moon party. ✉ *81600 Overseas Hwy. (MM 81 BS), Upper Matecumbe Key* ☎ *305/664–0604* ⊕ *www.moradabay-restaurant.com* 🖃 *AE, D, MC, V.*

★ **Fodor's**Choice ✕ **Pierre's.** *French.* One of the Keys' most elegant
$$$$ restaurants, Pierre's marries colonial style with modern food trends. Full of interesting architectural artifacts, the place oozes style, especially the wicker chair–strewn veranda overlooking the bay. Save your best "tropical chic" duds for dinner here, so you don't stand out from your surroundings. The food, drawn from French and Floridian influences, is multilayered and beautifully presented. Among the appetizer choices, few can resist the lamb ravioli or shrimp bisque. A changing list of entrées might include hogfish meunière and pan-seared duck breast with caramelized sweet potatoes. The downstairs bar is a perfect spot for catching sunsets, sipping martinis, and enjoying light eats. If you're lucky, catch a full-moon party with bonfires and live music. ✉ *81600 Overseas Hwy. (MM 81.5 BS), Upper Matecumbe Key* ☎ *305/664–3225* ⊕ *www.pierres-restaurant.com* ⌕ *Reservations essential* 🖃 *AE, D, DC, MC, V* ⊗ *No lunch.*

$$$ ✕ **Uncle's Restaurant.** *Italian.* Former fishing guide and current chef Joe LePree adds flair to standard seafood dishes by expanding the usual grilled, broiled, or blackened options. Here you can also have your seafood almandine, *Milanese* (breaded and fried), or *LePree* (with artichokes, mushrooms, and lemon-butter wine sauce). You also can feast on mussels or littleneck clams in a marinara or garlic sauce. Specials sometimes combine game (bison, caribou, or elk) with seafood. Portions are huge, so share dishes or take home a doggie bag, or order off the $13.95 light menu. Weather permitting, sit outdoors in the garden; poor acoustics make dining indoors unusually noisy. ✉ *80900 Overseas Hwy. (MM 81 OS), Upper Matecumbe*

Key ☎ *305/664–4402* ⊕ *www.unclesrestaurant.com* ⊟ *AE,*
D, DC, MC, V ⊗ *Closed Mon.*

WHERE TO STAY

2

★ Fodor'sChoice ☒ **Casa Morada.** This relic from the 1950s was
$$$$ rescued and restyled into a suave, design-forward, all-suites
property in 2000. Subsequent renovations have added
outdoor showers and Jacuzzis to some of the suites, each
of which claims its own design personality, many with an
Asian feel. Lush landscaping, a pool surrounded by a sandy
"beach" on its own island accessible by a bridge, and lounge
chairs at the water's edge lend a spalike vibe; complimentary
yoga classes, a Zen garden, and a rock waterfall complete
the scene. Cool tile-and-terrazzo floors invite you to kick off
your shoes and step out onto your private patio overlooking the gardens and the bay. Breakfast and lunch are served
on the waterside terrace. **Pros:** cool design; complimentary
snacks and bottled water; complimentary use of bikes, kayaks, and snorkel gear. **Cons:** trailer park across the street;
beach is small and inconsequential. ✉ *136 Madeira Rd.*
(MM 82 BS), Upper Matecumbe Key ☎ *305/664–0044 or*
888/881–3030 ⊕ *www.casamorada.com* ⇆ *16 suites* ⌂ *In-*
room: a/c, safe, DVD, Wi-Fi. In-hotel: restaurant, room
service, bar, pool, water sports, bicycles, laundry service,
no kids under 16 ⊟ *AE, MC, V* ⦿ *CP.*

$$$$ ☒ **Cheeca Lodge & Spa.** Newly renovated after a fire closed
★ it down for a year, Cheeca came back better than ever
in December 2009. The fire demolished its historic main
lodge, but in its place are West Indian–style rooms boasting
luxurious touches like elegant balcony tubs that fill from
the ceiling. If soaking in the tub is not your thing, soak in
the great views from the updated showers. The renovation
includes a newly formatted main dining room plus a sushi
bar and an upgraded swimming pool with underwater
speakers and new tiki bar. The resort's other buildings have
remained much as they were, but the spa got a face-lift
with the addition of mud baths, an adults-only lap pool,
and a fitness center. For families, there's the 1,200-foot
private beach, a nature trail, and Camp Cheeca—a fun
and educational program that makes use of a playground.
Golf (nine holes), tennis, and all manner of water sports
cater to sports enthusiasts. **Pros:** beautifully landscaped
grounds; new designer rooms; plenty of activities. **Cons:**
expensive rates; $39 resort fee for activities; busy. ✉ *81801*
Overseas Hwy. (MM 82 OS, Box 527), Upper Matecumbe

Key ☎305/664–4651 or 800/327–2888 ⊕www.cheeca. com ⬩214 rooms, 44 1-bedroom suites, 4 2-bedroom suites ⬩In-room: a/c, safe, kitchen (some) refrigerator, DVD, Wi-Fi. In-hotel: 2 restaurants, room service, bar, golf course, tennis courts, pools, gym, spa, beachfront, diving, water sports, bicycles, children's programs (ages 5–12), laundry service, Wi-Fi hotspot ☰AE, D, DC, MC, V.

$$$$ ☷ **Chesapeake Beach Resort.** This boutique hotel was renovated in 2007 with modern conveniences, but keeps its retro look. High-tech gadgets like flat-screen TVs, CD players, and MP3 players give the place an up-to-date feel. Coral stone and dark wood accent the rooms, each of which has a porch or a balcony. Most units are lined up along the long stretch of sand that all but encircles a lagoon; others overlook the tennis court. **Pros:** oceanfront location; free use of water-sports equipment. **Cons:** dated exterior; mandatory $18 resort fee (per room per night). ✉83409 Overseas Hwy. (MM 83.5 OS), Upper Matecumbe Key ☎305/664–4662 or 800/338–3395 ⊕www.chesapeake-resort.com ⬩44 rooms, 8 suites, 13 villas ⬩In-room: a/c, kitchen (some), Wi-Fi. In-hotel: tennis court, pools, gym, beachfront, water sports, bicycles, laundry facilities, some pets allowed ☰AE, D, MC, V ▢CP.

$$–$$$ ☷ **Drop Anchor Resort and Marina.** It's easy to find your cottage here, as they are painted in an array of Crayola colors. Immaculately maintained, this place has the feel of an old friend's beach house. Inside you'll find soothing West Indies–type furnishings and kitschy-cool, 1950s-era tile in the bathrooms. Welcoming as the rooms may be, you didn't come to the Keys to sit indoors: there's a luscious expanse of white sand awaiting, and you can catch ocean breezes from either your balcony, a comfy Adirondack chair, or a picnic table perched in the sand. There's a boat ramp to accommodate anglers. **Pros:** bright and colorful; attention to detail; laid-back charm. **Cons:** noise from the highway; beach is better for fishing than swimming. ✉84959 Overseas Hwy. (MM 85 OS), Windley Key ☎305/664–4863 or 888/664–4863 ⊕www.dropanchorresort.com ⬩18 suites ⬩In-room: a/c, kitchen (some), refrigerator. In-hotel: pool, beachfront, laundry facilities ☰AE, D, DC, MC, V.

$$$$ ☷ **The Islander Resort.** Although the vintage sign is straight out of a *Happy Days* rerun, this property has undergone a top-to-bottom transformation, while the general layout retained a 1950s feel. The decor is modern and yet comfortable, with white cottage-style furnishings, elegant fabrics, and sunny yellow bedrooms. Private screened porches lead to a coral-shell oceanfront beach with palm trees bending in the sea breeze. Families snap up suites in the oceanfront Beach House; couples looking for more privacy head to rooms set back from the beach. The pools—one saltwater, one freshwater—earn high marks, as do the full kitchens. A 200-foot dock, lighted at night, plus shuffleboard, basketball, and volleyball, add to the resort feel. **Pros:** spacious rooms; nice kitchens; eye-popping views. **Cons:** pricey for what you get; beach has rough sand; no a/c in the screened gym. ⊠ *82200 Overseas Hwy. (MM 82.1 OS), Upper Matecumbe Key* ☎ *305/664–2031 or 800/753–6002* ⊕ *www.islanderfloridakeys.com* ⤳ *114 rooms* ⌂ *In-room: a/c, safe, kitchen, Wi-Fi. In-hotel: restaurant, bar, pools, gym, beachfront, water sports, bicycles, laundry facilities, Wi-Fi hotspot, some pets allowed* ⊟ *AE, D, DC, MC, V* � *CP.*

★ **Fodor's**Choice ⊡ **The Moorings Village.** This tropical retreat is
$$$$ everything you imagine when you think of the Keys—from hammocks swaying between towering trees to sugar-white sand (arguably the Keys' best resort beach) lapped by aqua-green waves. West Indies–style cottages with cypress and Dade County pine accents, colorful shutters, private verandas, and wicker furniture sit in a canopy of coconut palms and old-forest landscaping on a residential street off the highway. This is a high-end slice of Old Florida, so don't expect tacky tiki bars. The one-, two-, and three-bedroom cottages all have modern kitchens with modern appliances. A palm-lined walkway leads to the beach, where a swimming dock awaits. During busy season there may be a two-night minimum-stay requirement for one-bedroom cottages, and a one-week minimum on other lodgings. The Moorings is possibly the most beautiful property in the Keys. **Pros:** romantic setting; good dining options with room-charging privileges; beautiful beach. **Cons:** minimum-night stays; no room service; extra fee for housekeeping; daily resort fee for activities. ⊠ *123 Beach Rd. (MM 81.6 OS), Upper Matecumbe Key* ☎ *305/664–4708* ⊕ *www.the-mooringsvillage.com* ⤳ *18 cottages and houses* ⌂ *In-room: a/c, kitchen, Wi-Fi. In-hotel: tennis court, pool, gym, spa, beachfront, water sports, laundry facilities, Wi-Fi hotspot* ⊟ *AE, D, MC, V.*

$ ⊡ **Ragged Edge Resort.** Tucked away in a residential area at the ocean's edge, this hotel is big on value but short on style. Ragged Edge draws returning guests who would rather fish off the dock and hoist a brew than loll around in Egyptian cotton sheets. Even those who turn their noses up at the cheap plastic deck furniture and pine paneling admit that the place has a million-dollar setting, with fabulous ocean views all around. There's no beach to speak of, but you can ride a bike across the street to Islamorada Founder's Park, where you'll find a nice little beach and water toys for rent. If a bit of partying puts you off, look elsewhere. Although the rooms are plain-Jane, they are clean and fairly spacious. Ground-floor units have screened porches; upper units have large decks, more windows, and beam ceilings. **Pros:** ocean-front location; boat docks and ramp; cheap rates. **Cons:** dated decor; guests can be noisy. ⊠ *243 Treasure Harbor Rd. (MM 86.5 OS), Plantation Key* ☎ *305/852–5389 or 800/436–2023* ⊕ *www.ragged-edge.com* ⌂ *10 units* ⟨ *In-room: a/c, kitchen (some), refrigerator, Wi-Fi. In-hotel: pool, bicycles, Wi-Fi hotspot* ⊟ *AE, MC, V.*

$$$ 🏨 **White Gate Court.** This small inn is a dog lover's paradise, with plenty of open space for pooches to play. All the sunny yellow cottages have beamed ceilings and spacious floor plans. The backyard has a barbecue and an umbrella-shaded table under palm trees. Rates include use of bicycles and a paddleboat. Boaters will appreciate the free docks and nearby offsite ramp. **Pros:** pet-friendly; homey feel; pretty trees. **Cons:** no pool; simple accommodations. ⊠ *76010 Overseas Hwy. (MM 76 BS), Upper Matecumbe Key* ☎ *305/664–4136 or 800/645–4283* ⊕ *www.white-gatecourt.com* ⌂ *7 units* ⟨ *In-room: a/c, kitchen, Wi-Fi. In-hotel: beachfront, water sports, bicycles, no elevator, laundry service, some pets allowed (fee)* ⊟ *MC, V.*

NIGHTLIFE

Islamorada is not known for its raging nightlife, but for local fun, Lorelei's is legendary. Others cater to the town's sophisticated clientele and fishing fervor.

Hog Heaven (⊠ *85361 Overseas Hwy. [MM 85.3 OS], Windley Key* ☎ *305/664–9669*) is a lively sports bar with three satellite dishes channeling the big game. These give way on weekends to a DJ or live bands.

Locals often refer to **Safari Lounge** (⊠ *73814 Overseas Hwy. [MM 73.5 OS], Lower Matecumbe Key* ☎ *305/664–8142*) as the Dead Animal Bar, or simply DAB, because of the mounted big-game trophies lining walls and the ceiling. Within eyeshot of the sea, it's a good spot to hoist a few with the island drinking crowd.

★ Behind a larger-than-life mermaid, the **Lorelei Restaurant & Cabana Bar** (⊠ *81924 Overseas Hwy. [MM 82 BS], Upper*

Matecumbe Key ☎ *305/664–2692* ⊕ *www.loreleifloridakeys. com*) is the kind of place you fantasize about during those long, cold winters up north. It's all about good drinks, tasty pub grub, and sherbet-hued sunsets set to live bands playing island tunes and light rock.

Zane Grey Long Key Lounge (☒ *81576 Overseas Hwy. [MM 81.5, BS], Upper Matecumbe Key* ☎ *305/664–4615*), above the World Wide Sportsman, was created to honor writer Zane Grey, one of the most famous members of the Long Key Fishing Club. The lounge displays the author's photographs, books, and memorabilia. Listen to live blues, jazz, and Motown on a wide veranda that invites sunset watching.

Ziggie & Mad Dog's (☒ *83000 Overseas Hwy. [MM 83 BS], Upper Matecumbe Key* ☎ *305/664–3391* ⊕ *www.ziggiesand-maddogs.com*), the area's glam celebrity hangout, serves appetizers with its happy-hour drink specials.

SPORTS AND THE OUTDOORS

BOATING

Marinas pop up every mile or so in the Islamorada area, so finding a rental or tour is no problem. Robbie's Marina is a prime example of a salty spot where you can find it all—from fishing charters and kayaking rentals to lunch and tarpon feeding.

Bump & Jump (☒ *81197 Overseas Hwy. [MM 81.2 OS], Upper Matecumbe Key* ☎ *305/664–9404 or 877/453–9463* ⊕ *www.keysboatrental.com*) is a one-stop shop for windsurfing, sailboat and powerboat rentals, sales, and lessons. This company delivers to your hotel or house, or drops it off right at the beach.

Founder's Park Watersports (☒ *MM 87 BS, Plantation Key* ☎ *305/434–8984* ⊕ *www.the-helm.com*) operates out of Islamorada Founder's Park. Hobie Wave sailboats are available, as are pedal boats and kayaks. Lessons range from a one-hour classes to race coaching.

See the islands from the comfort of your own boat (captain's cap optional) when you rent from **Houseboat Vacations of the Florida Keys** (☒ *85944 Overseas Hwy. [MM 85.9 BS], Plantation Key* ☎ *305/664–4009* ⊕ *www.floridakeys. com/houseboats*). The company maintains a fleet of 42- to 55-foot boats that accommodate up to 10 people and come outfitted with everything you need besides food.

(You may provision yourself at a nearby grocery store.) The three-day minimum starts at $1,112; one week costs $1,950 and up. Kayaks, canoes, and skiffs suitable for the ocean are also available.

Electric boats offer a noise-free, fume-free alternative. The earth-friendly **Islamorada Queen** (⊠ *Robbie's Marina [MM 77.5 BS], Lower Matecumbe Key* ☎ *305/360–0804*) offers two-hour backcountry and sunset excursions that start at $39 per person. Historical excursions to Lignumvitae Key State Park are also popular.

Can't decide between a limo and a yacht? Do both aboard the **Nauti-Limo** (⊠ *Lorelei Restaurant & Yacht Club [MM 82 BS], Upper Matecumbe Key* ☎ *305/942–3793* ⊕ *www.nautilimo.com*). Captain Joe Fox has converted the design of a 1983 pink Caddy stretch limo into a less-than-luxurious but certainly curious watercraft. One-hour tours start at $65 per couple. The seaworthy hybrid—complete with wheels—can sail topless if you're in the mood to let it all hang out. Only in the Keys!

Robbie's Boat Rentals & Charters (⊠ *77522 Overseas Hwy. [MM 77.5 BS], Lower Matecumbe Key* ☎ *305/664–9814 or 877/664–8498* ⊕ *www.robbies.com*) does it all. The company will give you a crash course on how not to crash your boat. The rental fleet includes an 18-foot skiff with a 60-horsepower outboard for $150 for four hours and $200 for the day to a 23-foot deck boat with a 130-horsepower engine for $185 for a half day and $235 for eight hours. Robbie's also rents fishing and snorkeling gear (there's good snorkeling nearby) and sells bait, drinks and snacks, and gas. Want to hire a guide who knows the local waters and where the fish lurk? Robbie's offers offshore fishing trips, patch-reef trips, and party-boat fishing. Backcountry flats trips are a specialty.

Captains Pam and Pete Anderson of **Treasure Harbor Marine** (⊠ *200 Treasure Harbor Dr. [MM 86.5 OS], Plantation Key* ☎ *305/852–2458 or 800/352–2628* ⊕ *www.treasureharbor.com*) provide everything you'll need for a vacation at sea. Best of all, they give excellent advice on where to find the best anchorages, snorkeling spots, or lobstering sites. Rental vessels range from a 23.5-foot Hunter to a 41-foot Morgan Out Island. Rates start at $160 a day, $700 a week. Hire a captain for $150–$200 a day. Marina facilities are basic—water, electric, laundry, picnic tables, and restrooms with showers. A store sells snacks, beverages, and sundries.

FISHING

Here in the self-proclaimed "Sportfishing Capital of the World," sailfish is the prime catch in the winter and *dolphinfish* (mahimahi) in the summer. Buchanan Bank just south of Islamorada is a good spot to try for tarpon in the spring. Blackfin tuna and amberjack are generally plentiful in the area, too. ■ TIP→ **The Hump at Islamorada ranks highest among anglers' favorite fishing spots in Florida (declared Florida Monthly magazine's best for seven years in a row) due to the incredible offshore marine life.**

Captain Ted Wilson (⊠ *Bud n' Mary's Marina, 79851 Overseas Hwy. [MM 79.9 OS], Upper Matecumbe Key* ☎ *305/942–5224 or 305/664–9463* ⊕ *www.captaintedwilson.com*) takes you into the backcountry for bonefish, tarpon, redfish, snook, and shark aboard a 17-foot boat that accommodates up to three anglers. For two people, half-day trips run $375, full-day trips $550, two-hour sunset bonefishing $225, and evening excursions $400. There's a $100 charge for an extra person.

Long before fly-fishing became popular, Sandy Moret was fishing the Keys for bonefish, tarpon, and redfish. Now he attracts anglers from around the world with the **Florida Keys Outfitters** (⊠ *Green Turtle, 81219 Overseas Hwy. [MM 81.2], Upper Matecumbe Key* ☎ *305/664–5423* ⊕ *www.floridakeysoutfitters.com*). Weekend fly-fishing classes, which include classroom instruction, equipment, and daily lunch, cost $985. Add $1,070 for two additional days of fishing. Guided fishing trips cost $395 for a half day, $535 for a full day. Packages combining fishing and accommodations at Islander Resort are available.

The 65-foot party boat *Miss Islamorada* (⊠ *Bud n' Mary's Marina, 79851 Overseas Hwy. [MM 79.8 OS], Upper Matecumbe Key* ☎ *305/664–2461 or 800/742–7945*) has full-day trips for $60. Bring your lunch, or buy one from the dockside deli.

★ Captain Ken Knudsen of the **Hubba Hubba Charters** (⊠ *MM 79.8 OS, Upper Matecumbe Key* ☎ *305/664–9281* ⊕ *www.capthubbahubba.com*) quietly poles his flatboat through the shallow water, barely making a ripple. Then he points and his clients cast. Five seconds later there's a zing, and the excitement of bringing in a snook, redfish, trout, or tarpon begins. Knudsen has fished Keys waters for more than 40 years. Now a licensed backcountry guide, he's ranked among Florida's top 10 by national fishing magazines. He offers four-hour sunset trips for tarpon ($425) and two-hour sunset trips for bonefish ($200), as well as half- ($375) and full-day ($550) outings. Prices are for one or two anglers, and tackle and bait (except for tarpon fishing) are included.

Like other top fly-fishing and light-tackle guides, Captain Geoff Colmes of **Fishabout Charters** (✉ *105 Palm La., Upper Matecumbe Key* ☎ *305/853–0741 or 800/741–5955* ⊕ *www. floridakeysflyfish.com*) helps his clients land trophy fish in the waters around the Keys ($500 to $550). But unlike the others, he also heads across Florida Bay to fish the coastal Everglades on three- and four-day trips (from $695 per angler) off his 65-foot mother ship, the *Fishabout*. It has four staterooms, private baths, living room, kitchen, satellite TV, and separate crew quarters. It's ideal when cold, windy weather shuts out fishing around the Keys. Rates include captain, crew, guide fees, lodging, all meals, tackle, and use of canoes for getting deep into shallow Everglades inlets.

SCUBA DIVING AND SNORKELING

About 1¼ nautical mi south of Indian Key is the **San Pedro Underwater Archaeological Preserve State Park**, which includes the wreck of a Spanish treasure-fleet ship that sank in 1733. The state of Florida protects the site for divers; no spearfishing or souvenir collecting is allowed. Resting in only 18 feet of water, its ruins are visible to snorkelers as well as divers, and attract a colorful array of fish.

Florida Keys Dive Center (✉ *90451 Overseas Hwy. [MM 90.5 OS], Plantation Key* ☎ *305/852–4599 or 800/433–8946* ⊕ *www.floridakeysdivectr.com*) organizes dives and snorkeling from John Pennekamp Coral Reef State Park to Alligator Light. The center has two 46-foot Coast Guard–approved dive boats, offers scuba training, and is one of the few Keys dive centers to offer nitrox and trimix (mixed gas) diving. Two-tank dives cost $74; half-day snorkeling is $35.

With a resort, pool, restaurant, lessons, and twice-daily dive and snorkel trips, **Holiday Isle Dive Shop** (✉ *84001 Overseas Hwy. [MM 84 OS], Windley Key* ☎ *305/664–3483 or 800/327–7070* ⊕ *www.diveholidayisle.com*) is a one-stop dive shop. Rates start at $50 for a two-tank dive without equipment.

TENNIS

Not all Keys recreation is on the water. Play tennis year-round at the **Islamorada Tennis Club** (⊠ *76800 Overseas Hwy. [MM 76.8 BS], Upper Matecumbe Key* ☎ *305/664–5341* ⊕ *islamoradatennisclub.net*). It's a well-run facility with four clay and two hard courts (all lighted), same-day racket stringing, ball machines, private lessons, and a full-service pro shop. Rates are from $25 a day.

WATER SPORTS

Florida Keys Kayak (⊠ *Robbie's Marina, 77522 Overseas Hwy. [MM 77.5 BS], Lower Matecumbe Key* ☎ *305/664–4878* ⊕ *www.kayakthefloridakeys.com*) rents kayaks for trips to Indian and Lignumvitae keys, two favorite destinations for paddlers. Kayak rental half-day rates (and you'll need plenty of time to explore those mangrove canopies) are $40 for a single kayak and $55 for a double. Pedal kayaks are available for $50 single and $65 double. The company also offers guided three-hour tours, including a snorkel trip to Indian Key ($45 per person). It also rents stand-up paddleboards, at $50 for a half-day including lessons, and canoes.

SHOPPING

Art galleries, upscale gift shops, and the mammoth World Wide Sportsman (if you want to look the part of a local fisherman, you must wear a shirt from here) make up the variety and superior style of Islamorada shopping.

BOOKS

Among the best buys in town are the used best-sellers at **Hooked on Books** (⊠ *82681 Overseas Hwy. [MM 81.9 OS], Upper Matecumbe Key* ☎ *305/517–2602* ⊕ *www.hooked-onbooksfloridakeys.com*), which also sells new titles, audio-books, and CDs.

GALLERIES

The go-to destination for one-of-a-kind gifts is **Gallery Morada** (⊠ *81611 Old Hwy. [MM 81.6 OS], Upper Matecumbe Key* ☎ *305/664–3650* ⊕ *www.gallerymorada.com*), where blown-glass objects are beautifully displayed, as are the original sculptures, paintings, lithographs, and jewelry of top South Florida artists.

The **Rain Barrel** (⊠ *86700 Overseas Hwy. [MM 86.7 BS], Plantation Key* ☎ *305/852–3084*) is a natural and unhurried shopping showplace. Set in a tropical garden of shady trees, native shrubs, and orchids, the crafts village has shops with works by local and national artists and resident artists in studios, including John Hawver, noted for Florida landscapes and seascapes. The Main Gallery up front showcases the craftsmanship of the resident artisans, who create marine-inspired artwork as you watch.

The **Redbone Gallery** (✉ *200 Industrial Dr. [MM 81.5 OS], Upper Matecumbe Key* ☎ *305/664–2002* ⊕ *www.redbone. org*), one of the largest sportfishing–art galleries in Florida, stocks hand-stitched clothing and giftware, in addition to work by wood and bronze sculptors such as Kendall van Sant; watercolorists Chet Reneson, Jeanne Dobie, and Kathleen Denis; and painters C.D. Clarke and Tim Borski. Proceeds benefit cystic fibrosis research.

GIFTS

At the **Banyan Tree** (✉ *81197 Overseas Hwy. [MM 81.2 OS], Upper Matecumbe Key* ☎ *305/664–3433 or 877/453–9463* ⊕ *www.banyantreegarden.com*), a sharp-eyed husband-and-wife team successfully combine antiques and contemporary gifts for the home and garden with plants, pots, and trellises in a stylishly sophisticated indoor–outdoor setting.

Island Silver & Spice (✉ *81981 Overseas Hwy. [MM 82 OS], Upper Matecumbe Key* ☎ *305/664–2714*) has tropical-style furnishings, rugs, and home accessories. The shop also stocks women's and men's resort wear and a large jewelry selection with high-end watches and marine-theme pieces.

SPORTING GOODS

Former U.S. presidents, celebrities, and record holders beam alongside their catches in black-and-white photos on the walls at **World Wide Sportsman** (✉ *81576 Overseas Hwy. [MM 81.5 BS], Upper Matecumbe Key* ☎ *305/664–4615 or 800/327–2880*), a two-level retail center that sells upscale fishing equipment, resort clothing, sportfishing art, and other gifts. When you're tired of shopping, relax at the Zane Grey Long Key Lounge just above World Wide Sportsman.

LONG KEY

MM 70–65.5.

Long Key isn't a tourist hot spot, making it a favorite destination for those looking to avoid the masses and enjoy some natural history in the process.

EXPLORING

Long Key State Park. Come here for solitude, hiking, fishing, and camping. On the ocean side, the Golden Orb Trail leads to a boardwalk that cuts through the mangroves (may require some wading) and alongside a lagoon where waterfowl congregate (as do mosquitoes, so be prepared). The shorter Layton Trail leads to the bay on the other side of the road. A 1¼-mi canoe trail winds through a tidal lagoon, and a broad expanse of shallow grass flats is perfect for bonefishing. Bring a mask and snorkel to observe the marine life in the shallow water. The park is particularly popular with campers who long to stake their tent at the campground on a beach. In summer no-see-ums (local reference for biting sand flies) also love the beach, so again—be prepared. The picnic area is on the water, too, but lacking beach. Canoes rent for $10 per day, and kayak rentals start at $17 for a single for two hours, $21.50 for a double. ⊠ *67400 Overseas Hwy. (MM 67.5 OS)* ☎ *305/664–4815* ⊕ *www.floridastateparks.org/longkey* ⊇ *$4.50 for 1 person, $5.50 for 2 people, and 50¢ for each additional person in the group* ☉ *Daily 8–sunset.*

EN ROUTE. As you cross Long Key Channel, look beside you at the old **Long Key Viaduct**. The second-longest bridge on the former rail line, this 2-mi-long structure has 222 reinforced-concrete arches. The old bridge is popular with anglers, who fish off the sides day and night, and cyclists.

WHERE TO EAT AND STAY

$$ ✕**Little Italy.** *Italian.* It's your basic Italian joint that looks like it's been around forever. In 2009 the chef who once made the place locally famous returned with a standard-issue Italian menu, throwing in a few surprises like conch parmigiana and crawfish salad sandwich. The lunch and dinner menus offer plenty of variety—dishes include shrimp po'boy, steaks, and a fisherman's platter—but few can resist the pull of the pasta. (Maybe it's the garlicky aroma that permeates the place.) Breakfast draws 'em in with $3.95 specials. ⊠ *68500 Overseas Hwy. (MM 68.5 BS)* ☎ *305/664–4472* ▭ *AE, MC, V* ☉ *Closed Mon.*

$$ ▣ **Lime Tree Bay Resort.** Easy on the eye and the wallet, this 2½-acre resort on Florida Bay is far from the hustle and bustle of the larger islands. Walls are painted with faux finishes and display tropical art. The five apartments offer

stunning Gulf views, while four deluxe rooms have cathedral ceilings and skylights. The best bet for two couples traveling together or families is the upstairs two-bedroom Tree House, with its covered porch and water views. Four off-site one-bedroom efficiencies are pet-friendly. Most units have a shared balcony or porch. Hammocks and chickee huts dot the gravelly beach. **Pros:** great views; friendly staff; close to Long Key State Park. **Cons:** only one restaurant nearby, shared balconies. ⊠ *68500 Overseas Hwy. (MM 68.5 BS), Layton* ☎ *305/664–4740 or 800/723–4519* ⊕ *www.limetreebayresort.com* ⇖ *10 rooms, 10 studios, 8 suites, 5 apartments, 4 efficiencies* ☼ *In-room: a/c, kitchen (some), refrigerator, Wi-Fi. In-hotel: tennis court, pool, beachfront, watersports, Wi-Fi hotspot, some pets allowed (fee)* ▭ *AE, D, DC, MC, V.*

¢ ⛰ **Long Key State Park.** Each of these oceanfront tent and RV
★ sites is right on the water, which is why they are booked so far in advance. You can—and should—reserve up to 11 months in advance, especially if you're planning a winter trip. By day you can try biking, hiking, boating, and fishing for bonefish, permit, and tarpon in the flats. Rangers lead guided walks and kayaking and canoeing excursions year-round. All sites have water and electricity. Fourteen days is the maximum stay. ☼ *Some pets allowed, flush toilets, partial hookups (electric and water), dump station, drinking water, showers, picnic tables, electricity, ranger station, swimming (ocean)* ⇖ *60 partial hookups (8 of the sites two-person tent-only)* ⊠ *67400 Overseas Hwy. (MM 67.5 OS)* ☎ *305/664–4815, 800/326–3521 (reservations)* ⊕ *www.reserveamerica.com* ▭ *AE, D, MC, V.*

The Middle Keys

WORD OF MOUTH

"Duck Key has some of the finer residential areas in the Keys. Duck is also the home of Hawk's Cay. It is midway between Islamorada and Marathon, maybe 20 minutes either way."

—stumpworks73

Updated
by Chelle
Koster
Walton

MOST OF THE ACTIVITY IN THE MIDDLE KEYS centers around the town of Marathon, the region's third-largest metropolitan area. On either end of it, smaller keys hold resorts, wildlife research and rehab facilities, a historic village, and a state park. The Middle Keys make a fitting transition from the Upper Keys to the Lower Keys not only geographically, but mentally. Crossing Seven Mile Bridge prepares you for the slow pace and don't-give-a-damn attitude you'll find a little farther down the highway. Fishing is one of the main attractions—in fact, the region's commercial fishing industry was founded here in the early 1800s. Diving is another popular pastime. There are also beaches and natural areas to enjoy in the Middle Keys, where mainland stress becomes an ever more distant memory.

ORIENTATION AND PLANNING

GETTING ORIENTED

If you get bridge fever—the heebie-jeebies when driving over long stretches of water—you may need a pair of blinders (or a couple of tranquilizers) before tackling the Middle Keys. Stretching from Conch Key to the far side of the Seven Mile Bridge, this zone is home to the region's two longest bridges: Long Key Viaduct and Seven Mile Bridge, both historic landmarks.

PLANNING

GETTING HERE AND AROUND

To get to the Middle Keys you can fly into either Miami International Airport or Key West International Airport. Key West is closer, but there are far fewer flights coming in and going out. Rental cars are available at both airports. Additionally, there is bus service from the Key West airport, $3 one-way with Keys Transit. The SuperShuttle charges $250 for up to 10 passengers from Miami International Airport to Big Pine Key.

U.S. 1 takes you from one end of the region to the other in a direct line that takes in most of the sights, but you'll find some interesting resorts and restaurants off the main drag.

ESSENTIALS

Transportation Contacts **City of Key West Department of Transportation Key West Transit** (☎ 305/809–3910 ⊕ www.keywestcity. com). **SuperShuttle** (☎ 305/871–2000 ⊕ www.supershuttle.com).

TOP REASONS TO GO

■ **Crane Point.** Visit 63-acre Crane Point Museum, Nature Center & Historic Site in Marathon for a primer on local natural and social history.

■ **A Beach for the Whole Family.** Sun, swim, and play with abandon at Marathon's family-oriented Sombrero Beach.

■ **Pigeon Key.** Step into the era of railroad building with a ferry ride to Pigeon Key's historic village, which was

once a residential camp for workers on Henry M. Flagler's Overseas Railroad.

■ **Dolphins.** Kiss a dolphin, and maybe even watch one paint, at Dolphin Research Center, which was begun by the maker of the movie *Flipper.*

■ **Fishing.** Anglers will be happy to hear that the deep-water fishing off Marathon is superb in both the bay and the ocean.

RESTAURANTS

Hope you're not tired of seafood, because the run of fish houses continues in the Middle Keys. In fact, Marathon boasts some of the best. Several are not so easy to find, but worth the search because of their local color and water views. Expect casual and friendly service with a side of sass. Restaurants may close for two to four weeks during the slow season between September and mid-November, so call ahead if you have a particular place in mind.

WHAT IT COSTS				
¢	$	$$	$$$	$$$$
RESTAURANTS				
under $10	$10–$15	$15–$20	$20–$30	over $30
HOTELS				
under $80	$80–$100	$100–$140	$140–$220	over $220

Restaurant prices are per person for a main course at dinner. Hotel prices are for a standard double room, excluding 6% sales tax (more in some counties) and 1%–4% tourist tax.

The Middle Keys

0   10 miles

0   10 km

Florida Bay

Seven Mile Bridge

Marathon
see detail map

Marathon Airport

Pigeon Key

Vaca Key

Grassy Key

Conch & Duck Keys

ATLANTIC OCEAN

HOTELS

From quaint old cottages to newly built town-house communities, the Middle Keys have it all, often with prices that are affordable than at the chain's extremes. Hawks Cay has the region's best selection of lodgings.

CONCH AND DUCK KEYS

MM 63–61.

This stretch of islands ranges from rustic fishing village to boating elite. Fishing dominates the economy, and many residents are descendants of immigrants from the mainland South. Across a causeway from the tiny fishing village of Conch Key is Duck Key, home to a more upscale community. There are a few lodging options here for those wanting to explore Marathon but avoid the traffic or take advantage of the water sports on Duck Key.

WHERE TO EAT AND STAY

$$$ ✕**Alma.** *Latin-American.* A refreshing escape from the
★ Middle Keys' same-old menus, Alma serves expertly pre-
pared Florida and Latin-Caribbean dishes in an elegant
setting. Take for instance the yellowtail snapper ceviche
with Peruvian popcorn, the divine calabaza squash and
lobster risotto, roasted breadfruit gnocchi, curried goat
stew with breadfruit tostones, and the grilled bone-in rib
eye. Finish your meal with the silky-smooth passionfruit
crème brûlée, which has just the right amount of tartness
to balance the delicate caramelized crust. ✉*Hawks Cay
Resort, 61 Hawks Cay Blvd., Duck Cay* ☎*305/743–7000
or 888/432–2242* ⊕*www.hawkscay.com* ▭*AE, D, DC,
MC, V* ⊘*No lunch.*

$$$ 🏨**Conch Key Cottages.** Some of the pastel-hued cottages here,
each named for a shell or sea creature and supplied with an
outdoor hammock, have a Bali theme. Continental breakfast is delivered to your door, and even better, each room
comes with a juicer and unlimited supply of oranges. The
best parts of the lodging—its secluded setting and man-
grove-framed beach—have endured through the decades.
Pros: far from the traffic noise; sandy beach; complimentary kayaks; lots of sunny decks and boat docks. **Cons:** far
from restaurants; some cottages are quite weathered; tiny
beach. ✉*62250 Overseas Hwy. (MM 62.3 OS), Conch Key*
☎*305/289–1377 or 800/330–1577* ⊕*www.conchkeycot-
tages.com* ⌘*9 cottages, 2 villas, 2 rooms* ⚷*In-room: a/c,
kitchen, Wi-Fi. In-hotel: pool, beachfront, Wi-Fi hotspot*
▭*AE, D, MC, V* ⦿*CP.*

★ **Fodor's Choice** 🏨**Hawks Cay Resort.** An in-the-water program
$$$– that lets you get up close and personal with dolphins makes
$$$$ this sprawling resort a family favorite. The 60-acre, Carib-
☯ bean-style retreat has plenty else to keep the kids occupied,
such as a pirate ship with water cannons at the kids' club,
where there are two family pools and air hockey. They
can also swim at one of the pools at the main lodge (the
other is adults-only) or in the protected saltwater lagoon.
When the older generation wants to head to the spa or out
to dinner at one of the restaurants, there are supervised
programs for kids up to age 12. The spacious rooms and
villas have a West Indies look. The room rate does not
include a $25 daily resort fee. **Pros:** huge rooms; restful
spa; full-service marina. **Cons:** no real beach; far from
Marathon's attractions. ✉*61 Hawks Cay Blvd. (MM 61
OS), Duck Key* ☎*305/743–7000 or 888/432–2242* ⊕*www.*

hawkscay.com ⌒ *161 rooms, 16 suites, 225 2 to 4–bedroom villas ☪ In-room: a/c, kitchen (some), refrigerator, Wi-Fi. In-hotel: 4 restaurants, room service, bars, tennis courts, pools, gym, spa, diving, water sports, children's programs (ages 5–12), laundry facilities, laundry service, concierge, Internet terminal, Wi-Fi hotspot, airport shuttle ═ AE, D, DC, MC, V. Elvis@cam-pr.com*

SPORTS AND THE OUTDOORS

DOLPHIN INTERACTION

Dolphin Connection (⊠ *Hawks Cay Resort, 61 Hawks Cay Blvd. [MM 61 OS], Duck Key* ☎ *888/313–5749* ⊕ *www. dolphinconnection.com*) offers three programs, including Dockside Dolphins, a 30-minute encounter from the dry training docks ($60); Dolphin Discovery, an in-water program that lasts about 45 minutes and lets you kiss, touch, and feed the dolphins ($155); and Trainer for a Day, a three-hour session with the animal training team ($295).

SCUBA AND SNORKELING

Dive Duck Key (⊠ *Hawks Cay Resort, 61 Hawks Cay Blvd. [MM 61 OS], Duck Key* ☎ *305/289–4931 or 877/386–3483* ⊕ *www.diveduckkey.com*) is a full-service dive shop offering rentals, charters, lessons, and certification courses. Snorkel trips cost $45. Scuba trips are $60 without gear and $75 to $115 with gear. Basic open-water certification courses require five days and cost $525. There's also Snuba, a snorkel-scuba hybrid where your tanks float on the surface rather than being attached to your back. Excursions start at $99.

WATER SPORTS

Sundance Watersports (⊠ *Hawks Cay Resort, 61 Hawks Cay Blvd.[MM 61 OS], Duck Key* ☎ *305/743–0145 Ext. 1925* ⊕ *www.sundancewatersports.net*) can take care of all your fun-on-the-water needs. Go on a one-hour guided Jet Ski tour ($149 for one to three people), soar on a parasail flight ($79 for single, $139 for tandem), go reef snorkeling ($44 including equipment rentals), or enjoy a catamaran snorkel trip ($35–$44) or sunset cruise ($42 each).

GRASSY KEY

MM 60–57.

Local lore has it that this sleepy little key was named not for its vegetation—mostly native trees and shrubs—but for an early settler by the name of Grassy. The key is primarily inhabited by a few families operating small fishing camps and roadside motels. There's no marked definition between it and Marathon, so it feels sort of like a suburb of its much larger neighbor to the south. Grassy Key's sights tend toward the natural, including a worthwhile dolphin attraction and a small state park.

GETTING HERE AND AROUND
Most visitors arriving by air drive to this destination either from Miami International Airport or Key West International Airport. Rental cars are readily available at both, and in the long run, are the most convenient means of transportation for getting here and touring around the Keys.

EXPLORING

Curry Hammock State Park. Looking for a slice of the Keys that's far removed from tiki bars? On the ocean and bay sides of the Overseas Highway, this park covers 1,000 acres of upland hammock, wetlands, and mangroves. On the bay side, across the street and 2 mi south of the entrance at MM 55.2, there's a trail through thick hardwoods to a rocky shoreline. The ocean side is more developed, with a sandy beach, a clean bathhouse, picnic tables, a playground, grills, and a gated 28-site campground. Locals consider the two paddling trails under canopies of arching mangroves among the best kayaking spots in the Keys. Rent a single for $17.20 or a double for $21.50 for two hours, or launch your own vessel. It's also a great spot for bird-watching. Herons, egrets, ibis, plovers, sanderlings, and occasionally raptors can be spotted; and if you're lucky, you may see a manatee swimming alongside your kayak. ⌧ *56200 Overseas Hwy. (MM 57 OS), Crawl Key* ☎ *305/289–2690* ⊕ *www.floridastateparks.org/curryhammock* ☎ *$4.50 for 1 person, $6 for 2, 50¢ per additional person* ☉ *Daily 8–sunset.*

☾ **Dolphin Research Center.** The 1963 movie *Flipper* popular-
★ ized the notion of humans interacting with dolphins, and Milton Santini, the film's creator, also opened this center, which is home to a colony of dolphins and sea lions. The nonprofit center has tours, narrated programs, and programs that allow you to greet the dolphins from dry land or play with them in their watery habitat. You can even paint a T-shirt with a dolphin—you pick the paint, the dolphin "designs" your shirt holding the paintbrush in its mouth

Close Encounters of the Flipper Kind

Here in the Florida Keys, where Milton Santini made the 1963 movie *Flipper*, close encounters of the mammalian kind are an everyday occurrence. There are a handful of facilities that allow you to commune with trained dolphins. In-water programs, where you actually swim with these intelligent creatures, are extremely popular, and require advance reservations. All programs begin with a course on dolphin physiology and behavior taught by a marine biologist. Afterward you learn a few important dos and don'ts (for example, don't wave your hands—you might, literally, send the wrong signal). Finally, you take the plunge.

For the in-water programs, the dolphins swim all around you. If you lie on your back with your feet out, they use their snouts to push you around. You can also grab a dorsal fin for an exciting ride. The in-water encounter lasts between 10 and 25 minutes, depending on the program. The entire experience takes about two hours. The best time to go is when it's warm, from March through October. You spend a lot of time in and out of the water, and you can feel your teeth chattering on a chilly day.

There's no need to get completely wet, however. Waterside programs let you feed, shake hands, and do tricks with dolphins from a submerged platform. These are great for people who aren't strong swimmers or for youngsters who don't meet a facility's minimum age requirements for in-water programs.

Possibilities include the Dolphin Connection in Duck Key, Dolphin Cove and Dolphins Plus in Key Largo (see ⇨ *Chapter 2, The Upper Keys*), and the Dolphin Research Center in Grassy Key.

($55). The center also offers programs for children and adults with disabilities. ⊠ *58901 Overseas Hwy. (MM 59 BS)* ☎ *305/289–1121 or 305/289–0002* ⊕ *www.dolphins. org* ☝ *$19.50* ☉ *Daily 9–4:30.*

WHERE TO EAT AND STAY

$$$$ ✕ **Hideaway Cafe.** *French.* The name says it all. Tucked between Grassy Key and Marathon, it's easy to miss if you're barnstorming through the Middle Islands. When you find it upstairs at Rainbow Bend Resort, you'll discover a favorite of locals who appreciate a well-planned menu, lovely ocean view, and quiet evening away from the crowds. For starters, dig into escargots à la Edison (sautéed with vegetables, pepper, cognac, and cream). Then feast on specialties such as a rarely found chateaubriand for one person, a whole roasted duck, or the seafood medley combining the catch of the day with scallops and shrimp in a savory sauce. Breakfast specials include a shrimp Florentine omelet, lox and eggs, and blueberry pancakes. ⊠ *Rainbow Bend Resort, 57784 Overseas Hwy. (MM 58 OS), Grassy Key* ☎ *305/289–1554 Ext. 400* ⊕ *www.hideawaycafe.com* ⊟ *AE, MC, V* ⊘ *No lunch.*

$–$$ ☷ **Bonefish Resort.** On a skinny lot bedecked with palm and banana trees, this motel-style hideaway is the best choice among the island's back-to-basics properties. It's not fancy, but it's cheap, clean, and a good base for paddling a kayak, wading for bonefish, and watching the waves roll in from a lounge chair. Rooms are decorated with tropical motifs like the colorful metal lizards on the doors. A narrow gravel courtyard lined with umbrella-shaded tables leads to a small beach and a waterfront pool. The kayaks and paddleboats encourage exploration of the waterfront. The communal deck is scattered with hammocks and chaises. Check-in is at next-door sister property Yellowtail Inn, which has cottages and efficiencies. **Pros:** decent price for the location; ocean-side setting. **Cons:** decks are small; simple decor. ⊠ *58070 Overseas Hwy. (MM 58 OS)* ☎ *305/743–7107 or 800/274–9949* ⊕ *www.bonefishresort.com* ⇨ *3 rooms, 11 efficiencies* ⚸ *In-room: a/c, kitchen (some), refrigerator, Wi-Fi. In-hotel: beachfront, bicycles, laundry facilities, Wi-Fi hotspot, some pets allowed* ⊟ *D, MC, V.*

$$–$$$ ☷ **Gulf View Waterfront Resort.** With a flock of 15 caged birds, ☾ a tortoise, and an iguana on the property, this homey duplex is part resort, part menagerie. Owner-occupied, the Gulf View's units are individually decorated with simple wicker furniture, tropical pastels, and ceiling fans. The one jarring design note is the green concrete foundation supporting the elevated swimming pool. Guests—mostly couples during the winter and families during holidays—appreciate the close proximity to the Dolphin Research Center, practically next door. (The resort offers discount passes to it and other nearby attractions.) Free use of canoes, paddleboats, kayaks, boat dock and ramp, and barbecue grills is also available for guests. **Pros:** parklike setting; sandy beach area with hammocks; close to restaurants. **Cons:** no elevator to office and second-story accommodations; some traffic noise. ⊠ *58743 Overseas Hwy. (MM 58.5 BS)* ☎ *305/289–1414 or 877/289–0111* ⊕ *www.gulfviewwaterfrontresort. com* ⇨ *2 rooms, 3 efficiencies, 3 1-bedroom apartments,*

3 2-bedroom apartments ⟡ In-room: a/c, kitchen (some), refrigerator, Wi-Fi. In-hotel: pool, water sports, bicycles, laundry facilities, some pets allowed ▭ AE, D, MC, V.

MARATHON

MM 53–47.5.

New Englanders founded this former fishing village in the early 1800s. The community on Vaca Key subsequently served as a base for pirates, salvagers (also known as "wreckers"), spongers, and, later, Bahamian farmers who eked out a living growing cotton and other crops. More Bahamians arrived in the hope of finding work building the railroad. According to local lore, Marathon was renamed when a worker commented that it was a marathon task to position the tracks across the 6-mi-long island.

During the building on the railroad, Marathon developed a reputation for lawlessness that rivaled that of the Old West. It is said that to keep the rowdy workers from descending on Key West for their off-hours endeavors, residents would send boatloads of liquor up to Marathon. Needless to say, things have quieted down considerably since then.

Still, Marathon is a bustling town, at least compared to other communities in the Keys. As it leaves something to be desired in the charm department, Marathon may not be your first choice of places to stay, but water sports types will find plenty to enjoy, and its historic and natural attractions merit a visit. Surprisingly good dining options abound, so you'll definitely want to stop for a bite even if you're just passing through on the way to Key West.

Throughout the year, Marathon throws fishing tournaments (practically monthly), a huge seafood festival in March, and lighted boat parades around the holidays.

GETTING HERE AND AROUND

The SuperShuttle charges $102 per passenger for trips from Miami International Airport to the Upper Keys. To go farther into the Keys, you must book an entire 11-person van, which costs about $250 to Marathon. For a trip to the airport, place your request 24 hours in advance.

Miami Dade Transit provides daily bus service from MM 50 in Marathon to the Florida City Wal-Mart Supercenter on the mainland. The bus stops at major shopping centers as well as on-demand anywhere along the route during daily round trips on the hour from 6 AM to 10 PM. The cost is $2 one way, exact change required. The Lower Keys Shuttle bus runs from Marathon to Key West ($3 one way), with scheduled stops along the way.

ESSENTIALS

Transportation Contacts **Lower Keys Shuttle** (☎ 305/809–3910 ⊕ www.kwtransit.com). **Miami Dade Transit** (formerly the Dade–Monroe Express ☎ 305/770–3131). **SuperShuttle** (☎ 305/871–2000 ⊕ www.supershuttle.com).

Visitor Information **Greater Marathon Chamber of Commerce and Visitor Center** (✉ 12222 Overseas Hwy. [MM 53.5 BS], Marathon ☎ 305/743–5417 or 800/262–7284 ⊕ www.floridakeysmarathon.com).

EXPLORING

Grassy Key segues into Marathon with little more than a slight increase in traffic and higher concentration of commercial establishments. Marathon's roots are anchored in fishing and boating, so look for marinas to find local color, fishing charters, and good restaurants. At its north end, Key Colony Beach is an old-fashioned island neighborhood worth a visit for its shops and restaurants. Nature lovers shouldn't miss the attractions on Crane Point. Other good places to leave the main road are at Sombrero Beach Road (MM 50), which leads to the beach, and 35th Street (MM 49), which takes you to a funky little marina and restaurant. U.S. 1 hightails through Hog Key and Knight Key before the big leap over Florida Bay and Hawk's Channel via the Seven Mile Bridge.

☾ **Crane Point Museum, Nature Center, and Historic Site.** Tucked
★ away from the highway behind a stand of trees, Crane Point—part of a 63-acre tract that contains the last-known undisturbed thatch-palm hammock—is delightfully undeveloped. This multiuse facility includes the **Museum of Natural History of the Florida Keys,** which has displays about local wildlife, a seashell exhibit, and a marine-life display with audio that makes you feel like you're at the bottom of the sea. Kids love the replica 17th-century galleon and pirate dress-up room where they can play, and the re-created **Cracker House** filled with insects, sea-turtle exhibits, and children's activities. On the 1-mi indigenous loop trail, visit the **Wild Bird Center** and the remnants of a Bahamian village, site of the restored **George Adderly House.** It is the

Marathon

KEY

- **1** *Restaurants*
- (1) *Hotels*
- ◿ *Dive Site*
- ⬟ *Boat Launch*

Conch Key

Duck Key

↗ TO
ISLAMORADA

Grassy Key

Crawl Key

Bamboo Key

Curry Hammock Park

◿ Thunderbolt

Coco Plum Dr.

Marathon Chamber of Commerce

Key Colony Bch

125 St.

117 St.

Walgreens

107 St.

110 St.

1

Golf Course

Marathon Post Office

100 St.

2 Key Colony Beach

Dolphin Dr.

Marathon Airport

83 St.

Marathon

Rd. St.

3

92 St.

Crane Point Museum at Crane Point Hammock

72 St.

The Turtle Hospital

4

63 St.

5

49 St.

Vaca Key

Gulf Terr. Ave

41 St.

(1)

39 St.

36 St.

(2)

⬟

Sombrero Beach

6

⬟

The American ◿

Boot Key Bridge

17 St.

7

Boot Key

Old Seven Mile Bridge

◆ Pigeon Key

Sombrero Reef ◿

Seven Mile Bridge

↙ TO
LOWER KEYS

Restaurants

Fish Tales Market and Eatery, **1**

Herbie's, **3**

Key Colony Inn, **2**

Keys Fisheries Market & Marina, **4**

Lazy Days South, **6**

Sunset Grille and Raw Bar, **7**

The Stuffed Pig, **5**

Hotels

Crystal Bay Resort & Marina, **1**

Tranquility Bay, **2**

oldest surviving example of Bahamian tabby (a concrete-like material created from sand and seashells) construction outside of Key West. A boardwalk crosses wetlands, rivers, and mangroves before ending at Adderly Village. From November to Easter docent-led tours are available; bring good walking shoes and bug repellent during warm weather. ⊠ *5550 Overseas Hwy. (MM 50.5 BS)* ☎ *305/743–9100* ⊕ *www.cranepoint.net* ☎ *$12* ⊘ *Mon.–Sat. 9–5, Sun. noon–5; call to arrange trail tours.*

NEED A BREAK? If you don't get a buzz from breathing in the robust aroma at **Leigh Ann's (More Than Just A) Coffee House** (⊠ **7537 Overseas Hwy. [MM 51.3 OS]** ☎ **305/743–2001** ⊕ **www. leighannscoffeehouse.com**), order an espresso shot, Cuban or Italian, for a satisfying jolt. Pastries are baked fresh daily, but the breakfast sandwich and Italian frittata cooked without added fat are among the big movers. Leigh Ann's also serves lunch—quiche and hot and cold sandwiches are on the menu. It's open weekdays 7–5, Saturday 7–3, and Sunday 8–noon.

★ **Pigeon Key.** There's much to like about this 5-acre island under the Old Seven Mile Bridge. You can reach it by walking across a 2.5-mi section of the bridge or by ferry. Once there, tour the island on your own or join a guided tour to explore the buildings that formed the early-20th-century work camp for the Overseas Railroad that linked the mainland to Key West. Later the island became a fish camp, a state park, and then government administration headquarters. Exhibits in a small museum recall the history of the Keys, the railroad, and railroad baron Henry M. Flagler. Pick up the ferry outside the gift shop, which occupies an old railroad car on Knight's Key (MM 47 OS), for a two-hour excursion. Ferry reservations are not required but recommended on weekends and during the busy winter season. ⊠ *1 Knights Key Blvd. (MM 45 OS), Pigeon Key* ☎ *305/289–0025 general information, 305/743–5999 tickets* ⊕ *www.pigeonkey.net* ☎ *$11* ⊘ *Office open daily 9:30–4; ferryboat departures at 10, 11:30, 1, and 2:30.*

Seven Mile Bridge. This is one of the most photographed images in the Keys. Actually measuring slightly less than 7 mi, it connects the Middle and Lower Keys, and is believed to be the world's longest segmental bridge. It has 39 expansion joints separating its various concrete sections. Each April runners gather in Marathon for the annual Seven

Mile Bridge Run. The expanse running parallel to Seven Mile Bridge is what remains of the **Old Seven Mile Bridge,** an engineering and architectural marvel in its day that's now on the National Register of Historic Places. Once proclaimed the Eighth Wonder of the World, it rested on a record 546 concrete piers. No cars are allowed on the old bridge today, but a 2.5-mi segment is open for biking, walking, and fishing.

★ **Sombrero Beach.** Here pleasant, shaded picnic areas overlook a coconut palm–lined grassy stretch and the Atlantic Ocean. Separate areas allow swimmers, boaters, and windsurfers to share the narrow cove. Facilities include barbecue grills, showers, and restrooms, as well as a large playground, a pier, and a volleyball court. Sunday afternoons draw lots of local families toting coolers. The park is accessible for those with disabilities and allows leashed pets. Turn east at the traffic light in Marathon and follow signs to the end. ⊠ *Sombrero Beach Rd. (MM 50 OS)* ☎ *305/743–0033* ⊜ *Free* ⊗ *Daily 8–sunset.*

☾ **The Turtle Hospital.** More than 100 injured sea turtles check in here and are later released every year. The 90-minute guided tours take you into recovery and surgical areas at the world's only state-certified veterinary hospital for sea turtles. In the "hospital bed" tanks, you can see recovering patients and others that are permanent residents due to their injuries. If you're lucky, you can visit hatchlings. Call ahead—tours are sometime cancelled due to medical emergencies. ⊠ *2396 Overseas Hwy. (MM 48.5 BS)* ☎ *305/743–2552* ⊕ *www.turtlehospital.org* ⊜ *$15* ⊗ *Daily 9–5; tours at 10, 1, 2, and 4.*

WHERE TO EAT

¢ ✕ **Fish Tales Market and Eatery.** *Seafood.* This roadside eatery with its own seafood market serves signature dishes such as oysters on a roll and catch of the day grilled on rye with coleslaw and melted Muenster cheese. You also can slurp lobster bisque or conch chowder. There are burgers, chicken, and dogs for those who don't do seafood. Plan to dine early; it's only open until 6:30 PM. This is a no-frills kind of place with a loyal local following, a couple of picnic tables, and friendly service. ⊠ *11711 Overseas Hwy. (MM 52.5 OS)* ☎ *305/743–9196 or 888/662–4822* ⊕ *www. floridalobster.com* ⊟ *AE, MC, V* ⊗ *Closed Sun.*

TURTLE TIME

Five species of threatened and endangered sea turtles frequent the waters of the Florida Keys. The **Loggerhead**, the most common, is named for the shape of its noggin. It grows to a heft of 300 pounds. It is the only one of the local turtles listed as threatened rather than endangered.

The vegetarian **Green Turtle** was once hunted for its meat, which has brought populations to their endangered stage. It can reach an impressive 500 pounds.

Named for the shape of its mouth, the **Hawksbill Turtle** is a relative lightweight at 150 pounds. It prefers rocks and reefs for habitat. The Keys are the only U.S. breeding site for the endangered critter.

The largest reptile alive, the **Leatherback Turtle** can weigh in at up to 2,000 pounds, attained from a diet of mainly jellyfish.

The rarest of local sea turtles, the **Kemps Ridley** is named after a Key West fisherman. A carnivore, it grows to 100 pounds.

The biggest threats to sea turtle survival include fibropapilloma tumors, monofilament fishing lines (which can sever their flippers), entanglement in ropes and nets, boat propeller run-ins, swallowing plastic bags (which appear to them as jellyfish), oil spills, and other human and natural impact.

$ ✕ **Herbie's.** *American.* Since 1972 this has been the go-to spot for quick and affordable comfort food, from homemade soup, cheeseburgers, and fried oysters to shrimp scampi, mussels marinara over pasta, and blackened chicken. You'll find all the local staples—conch, steamed shrimp, and fresh fish prepared blackened, broiled, grilled with butter, or chargrilled "au naturale"—to enjoy at picnic tables in the screened-in porch or inside where it's air-conditioned and the locals congregate in summer. ✉ *6350 Overseas Hwy. (MM 50.5 BS)* ☎*305/743–6373* ▭*No credit cards* ☉ *Closed Sun. and Mon.*

$$ ✕ **Key Colony Inn.** *Italian.* For lunch there are fish and steak entrées served with fries, salad, and bread in addition to sandwiches and Italian specialties. At dinner you can't miss with traditional dishes like veal Oscar and steak au poivre, or such specialties off the extensive menu as seafood Italiano (a dish of scallops and shrimp sautéed in garlic butter and served with marinara sauce over a bed of linguine). The place is renowned for its Sunday brunch, served from

November to April. ■TIP→ **Abide by the 25-MPH speed limit on Key Colony Beach, as it is heavily patrolled.** ⊠ *700 W. Ocean Dr. (MM 54 OS), Key Colony Beach* ☎ *305/743–0100* ⊕ *www.kcinn.com* ═ *AE, MC, V.*

$$
\begin{array}{l}
\text{\$\$} \\
\bigstar \\
\circlearrowleft
\end{array}
$$

$$ ⨉ $$ **Keys Fisheries Market & Marina.** *Seafood.* From the parking lot, this commercial warehouse flanked by fishing boats and lobster traps barely hints at the restaurant inside. Order at the window outside, pick up your food, then dine at one of the waterfront picnic tables outfitted with rolls of paper towels. Fresh seafood (and a token hamburger and chicken sandwich) are the only things on the menu. A huge lobster Reuben ($14.95) served on thick slices of toasted bread is the signature dish. Other delights include the shrimpburger, very rich whiskey-peppercorn snapper, and the Keys Kombo (broiled or grilled lobster, shrimp, scallops, and mahimahi for $29). There are also sushi, an eight-flavor ice-cream station, and a bar serving beer and wine. Kids like feeding the fish while they wait for their food. ⊠ *3390 Gulfview Ave. (turn west on 35th St.), end of 35th St. (MM 49 BS)* ☎ *305/743–4353 or 866/743–4353* ⊕ *www.keysfisheries.com* ═ *MC, V.*

$$ \text{\$\$\$} $$
$$ \bigstar $$ ⨉ **Lazy Days South.** *Seafood.* Tucked into Marathon Marina a half-mile north of the Seven Mile Bridge, the restaurant offers views just as spectacular as the highly lauded food. A spin-off of an Islamorada favorite, here you'll find a wide range of daily offerings from garlic-baked clams and a coconut-fried fish du jour sandwich to shrimp sautéed in garlic cream sauce and beef tips over rice. Choose a table on the outdoor deck, or inside underneath paddle fans and surrounded by local art. ⊠ *725 11th St. (MM 47.3 OS)* ☎ *306/289–0839* ⊕ *www.keysdining.com/lazydays* ═ *AE, D, MC, V.*

$$ c $$
$$ \bigstar $$ ⨉ **The Stuffed Pig.** *American.* With only eight tables and a counter inside, this breakfast-and-lunch place is always hopping. When the weather's right, grab a table out back. The kitchen whips up comfort food like burgers, subs, seafood platters, or pulled pork with hand-cut fries, but a quick glance around the room reveals that the all-day breakfast is the main draw. You can get the usual breakfast plates, but most newcomers opt for oddities like the lobster omelet, alligator tail and eggs, or "grits and grunts" (that's fish, to the rest of us). ⊠ *3520 Overseas Hwy. (MM 49 BS)* ☎ *305/743–4059* ⊕ *www.thestuffedpig.com* ═ *No credit cards* ☉ *No dinner.*

$$ \text{\$\$\$} $$ ⨉ **Sunset Grille & Raw Bar.** *Seafood.* After a walk or bike ride along the Old Seven Mile Bridge, treat yourself to a

seafood lunch or dinner at this vaulted tiki hut under the bridge. For lunch, start with the conch chowder or fritters, and then move on to the Voodoo grouper sandwich topped with mango-guava mayo, and finish with a tasty key lime pie. Wear your swimsuit if you want to take a dip in the pool for a post-lunch swim. Dinner specialties add a creative twist, like the Brie-stuffed filet mignon, coconut curry lobster, and crab au gratin. ⊠ *7 Knights Key Blvd. (MM 47 OS)* ☎ *305/396–7235* ⊕ *www.sunsetgrille7milebridge. com* ⊟ *AE, D, MC, V*

WHERE TO STAY

$ ⬚ **Crystal Bay Resort & Marina.** This resort is a blast from the past. The retro motel has shuffleboard courts and a self-serve tiki bar. The paint is chipping on some of the widely spaced buildings, but the room decor looks modern with a few vintage touches. Of the selection of rooms and suites, Room 20 offers the best digs, with a bay view that goes on forever. We're told the Wright Brothers stayed in Unit 29—and who's to argue? The fish stories come fast and furious here. Many folks bring their boats and stay two or three weeks at a time. If all this sounds eccentrically charming to you, you'll have a grand old time here. **Pros:** nice kitchens in some rooms; friendly staff; casual atmosphere. **Cons:** some rooms need updating; steep charge for extra guests. ⊠ *4900 Overseas Hwy. (MM 49 BS)* ☎ *305/289–8089 or 888/289–8089* ⊕ *www.crystalbayresort.com* ⥀ *15 rooms, 15 efficiencies* ♺ *In-room: a/c, kitchen (some), refrigerator (some). In-hotel: tennis courts, water sports, Wi-Fi hotspot* ⊟ *D, MC, V.*

$$$$ ⬚ **Tranquility Bay.** The 87 two- and three-bedroom town
★ houses at this luxurious resort have gingerbread trim, white-
☺ picket fences, and open-floor-plan interiors decorated in trendy cottage style. The picture-perfect theme continues with the palm-fringed pool and the sandy beach edged with a ribbon of blue bay (and echoed in the blue-and-white stripes of the poolside umbrellas). Guests look like models on a photo shoot: attractive young families enjoying themselves at the sunny decks, casual outdoor bar, or elegant restaurant. **Pros:** secluded setting; gorgeous design; lovely crescent beach. **Cons:** a bit sterile; no real Keys atmosphere; cramped building layout. ⊠ *2600 Overseas Hwy. (MM 48.5 BS)* ☎ *305/289–0888 or 866/643–5397* ⊕ *www.tranquilitybay.com* ⥀ *45 2-bedroom suites, 41 3-bedroom suites* ♺ *In-room: a/c, kitchen, refrigerator, DVD, Wi-Fi. In-hotel:*

2 restaurants, bars, pools, gym, beachfront, diving, water sports, Internet terminal, Wi-Fi hotspot = *AE, D, MC, V.*

SPORTS AND THE OUTDOORS

BIKING

Tooling around on two wheels is a good way to see Marathon. There's easy cycling on a 1-mi off-road path that connects to the 2 mi of the Old Seven Mile Bridge leading to Pigeon Key.

"Have bikes, will deliver" could be the motto of **Bike Marathon Bike Rentals** (☎ *305/743–3204*), which gets beach cruisers to your hotel door for $45 per week, including a helmet. It's open Monday through Saturday 9–4 and Sunday 9–2.

Overseas Outfitters (✉ *1700 Overseas Hwy. [MM 48 BS]* ☎ *305/289–1670*) rents aluminum cruisers and hybrid bikes for $10 to $15 per day. The company also rents tandem bikes and children's bikes. It's open weekdays 9–6 and Saturday 9–3, Sunday 10–2.

BOATING

Sail, motor, or paddle: Whatever your choice of modes, boating is what the Keys is all about. Brave the Atlantic waves and reefs or explore the backcountry islands on the Gulf side. If you don't have a lot of boating and chart-reading experience, it's a good idea to tap into local knowledge on a charter.

Captain Pip's (✉ *1410 Overseas Hwy. [MM 47.5 OS]* ☎ *305/743–4403 or 800/707–1692* ⊕ *www.captainpips. com*) rents 19- to 24-foot outboards, $195–$330 per day, as well as tackle and snorkeling gear. You also can charter a small boat with a guide, $500–$550 for a half day and $750–$800 for a full day.

Fish 'n Fun (✉ *4590 Overseas Hwy. [MM 49.5 OS], at Banana Bay Resort & Marina* ☎ *305/743–2275 or 800/471–3440* ⊕ *www.fishnfunrentals.com*) lets you get out on the water in 19- to 26-foot powerboats starting at $140 for a half day, $190 for a full day. The company offers free delivery in the Middle Keys. You also can rent Jet Skis and kayaks.

For those who want a live-aboard vacation, **Florida Keys Bareboat Charters** (☎ *305/684–6902* ⊕ *www.floridakeysbareboatchartercompany.com*) rents 27-foot Catalina and Balboa sailboats for $250 a day, $800 a week. The fee includes home-port dockage.

FISHING

For recreational anglers, the deepwater fishing is superb in both bay and ocean. Marathon West Hump, one good spot, has depths ranging from 500 to more than 1,000 feet. Locals fish from a half-dozen bridges, including Long Key Bridge, the Old Seven Mile Bridge, and both ends of Tom's Harbor. Barracuda, bonefish, and tarpon all frequent local waters. Party boats and private charters are available.

★ Morning, afternoon, and night, fish for mahimahi, grouper, and other tasty catch aboard the 73-foot **Marathon Lady** (⊠ *MM 53 OS, at 117th St.* ☎ *305/743–5580* ⊕ *www. fishfloridakeys.com/marathonlady*), which departs on half-day ($45) excursions from the Vaca Cut Bridge, north of Marathon. Join the crew for night fishing ($55) from 6:30 to midnight from Memorial Day to Labor Day; it's especially beautiful on a full-moon night.

Captain Jim Purcell, a deep-sea specialist for ESPN's *The American Outdoorsman,* provides one of the best values in Keys fishing. **Sea Dog Charters** (⊠ *1248 Overseas Hwy. [MM 47.5 BS]* ☎ *305/743–8255* ⊕ *www.seadogcharters. net*), next to the Seven Mile Grill, has half- and full-day offshore, reef and wreck, and backcountry fishing trips, as well as fishing and snorkeling trips aboard 30- to 37-foot boats. The cost is $60 per person for a half day, regardless of whether your group fills the boat, and includes bait, light tackle, ice, coolers, and fishing licenses. If you prefer an all-day private charter on a 37-foot boat, he offers those, too, for $600 for up to six people. A fuel surcharge may apply.

GOLF

Key Colony Beach Golf & Tennis (⊠ *460 8th St. [MM 53.5 OS], Key Colony Beach* ☎ *305/289–9859* ⊕ *www.keycolony-beach.net/recreation.html*), a 9-hole course near Marathon, charges $11 for the course ($9 for each additional 9 holes), $3 per person for club rental, and $2 for a pull cart. There are no reserved tee times and there's no rush. Play from 7:30 AM to dusk. A little pro shop meets basic golf needs. Two lighted tennis courts are open from 7:30 AM to 10 PM.

SCUBA DIVING AND SNORKELING

Local dive operations take you to Sombrero Reef and Lighthouse, the most popular down-under destination in these parts. For a shallow dive and some lobster-nabbing, Coffins Patch, off Key Colony Beach, is a good choice. A number of wrecks such as *Thunderbolt* serve as artificial reefs. Many operations out of this area will also take you to Looe Key Reef.

Hall's Diving Center & Career Institute (✉ *1994 Overseas Hwy. [MM 48.5 BS]* ☎ *305/743–5929 or 800/331–4255* ⊕ *www. hallsdiving.com*) has been training divers for more than 40 years. Along with conventional twice-a-day snorkel and two-tank dive trips ($40–$55) to the reefs at Sombrero Lighthouse and wrecks like the *Thunderbolt,* the company has more unusual offerings like digital and video photography.

Twice daily, **Spirit Snorkeling** (✉ *1410 Overseas Hwy., Slip No. 1 [MM 47.5 BS]* ☎ *305/289–0614* ⊕ *www.spiritsnorkeling.net*) departs on snorkeling excursions to Sombrero Lighthouse Reef for $30 a head.

Tildens Scuba Center (✉ *4650 Overseas Hwy. [MM 49.5 BS], Marathon* ☎ *305/743–7255 or 888/728–2235* ⊕ *www.tildensscubacenter.com*) has been providing lessons, tours, gear rental, and daily snorkel and scuba adventures for the past 30 years. Snorkel cruises range from $36 to $61. Look for the large moray eel mural on the side of the building.

TOURS

Conch Air (✈ *Marathon Airport, Marathon 33050* ☎ *305/ 395–1117* ⊕ *www.conch-air.com*) specializes in romantic sunset flights. A 1935 Waco biplane for two passengers flies out of Marathon Airport; scenic rides start at $74 per person.

WATER SPORTS

For all your water-sports rental needs, **Jerry's Charter Service & Watersport Rentals** (✉ *Banana Bay Resort & Marina, 4590 Overseas Hwy. [MM 49.5 BS]* ☎ *305/289–7298 or 800/775–2646* ⊕ *www.jerryscharters.com*) is your one-stop place. It rents kayaks, Jet Skis, 14- to 25-foot day sailers, snorkel equipment, fishing rods, and power- and pontoon boats.

The Lower Keys

www.fodors.com/forums

Updated
by Chelle
Koster
Walton

BEGINNING AT BAHIA HONDA KEY, the islands of the Florida Keys become smaller, more clustered, and more numerous, a result of ancient tidal water flowing between the Florida Straits and the gulf. Here you're likely to see more birds and mangroves than other tourists, and more refuges, beaches, and campgrounds than museums, restaurants, and hotels. The islands are made up of two types of limestone, both denser than the highly permeable Key Largo limestone of the Upper Keys. As a result, fresh water forms in pools rather than percolating through the rock, creating watering holes that support alligators, snakes, deer, rabbits, raccoons, and migratory ducks. (Many of these animals can be seen in the National Key Deer Refuge on Big Pine Key.) Nature was generous with her beauty in the Lower Keys, which have both Looe Key Reef, arguably the Keys' most beautiful tract of coral, and Bahia Honda State Park, considered one of the best beaches in the world for its fine sand dunes, clear warm waters, and panoramic vista of bridges, hammocks, and azure sky and sea. Big Pine Key is fishing headquarters for a laid-back community that swells with retirees in the winter. South of it, the dribble of islands can flash by in a blink of an eye if you don't take the time to stop at a roadside eatery or check out tours and charters at the little marinas. They include Little Torch Key, Middle Torch Key, Ramrod Key, Summerland Key, Cudjoe Key, Sugarloaf Keys, and Saddlebunch Key. Lying offshore of Little Torch Key, Little Palm Island once welcomed U.S. presidents and other notables to its secluded fishing camp. It was also the location for the movie *PT 109* about John F. Kennedy's celebrated World War II heroism. Today it still offers respite to the upper class in the form of an exclusive getaway resort accessible only by boat.

ORIENTATION AND PLANNING

GETTING ORIENTED

In truth, the Lower Keys include Key West, but since it's covered in its own section and is as different from the rest of the Lower Keys as peanut butter is from jelly, this section covers just the keys between MM 37 and MM 9. The Seven Mile Bridge drops you into the lap of this homey, quiet part of the Keys.

Heed speed limits in these parts. They may seem incredibly strict, given that the traffic is lightest of anywhere in the

TOP REASONS TO GO

■ **Wildlife-viewing.** The Lower Keys are populated with all kinds of animals. Watch especially for Key deer but also other wildlife at the Blue Hole in National Key Deer Refuge.

■ **Bahia Honda Key State Park.** Explore the beach and trails, then camp for the night at this gorgeous state park.

■ **Kayaking.** Get out in a kayak to spot birds in the Keys' backcountry wildlife refuges.

■ **Snorkeling.** Grab a mask and fin and head to Looe Key Reef to see amazing coral formations and fish so bright and animated they look like cartoons.

■ **Fishing.** All kinds of fishing are great in the Lower Keys. Cast from a bridge, boat, or shoreline flats for bonefish, tarpon, and other feisty catches.

Keys, but the purpose is to protect the resident Key deer population, and officers of the law pay strict attention.

PLANNING

GETTING HERE AND AROUND

To get to the Lower Keys, fly into either Miami International Airport or Key West International Airport. Key West is closer, but there are far fewer flights coming in and going out. Rental cars are available at both airports. Additionally, there is bus service from the Key West airport; $3 one way with Keys Transit.

ESSENTIALS

Transportation Contacts **City of Key West Department of Transportation Key West Transit** (☎ 305/809–3910 ⊕ www. keywestcity.com).

RESTAURANTS

Restaurants are fewer and farther between in the Lower Keys, and you won't find the variety of offerings in eateries closer to Miami and in Key West. Mostly you'll find seafood joints where dinner is fresh off the hook and license plates or dollar bills stuck to the wall count for decor. For a special occasion, hop aboard the ferry at Little Torch Key to experience the globe-trotting cuisine of private Little Palm Island resort. Restaurants may close for a two- to four-week vacation during the slow season—between mid-September and mid-November.

HOTELS

Fishing lodges, dive resorts, and campgrounds are the most prevalent type of lodging in this part of the Keys. Rates are generally much lower than on other Keys, especially Key West, which makes this a good place to stay if you're on a budget.

WHAT IT COSTS				
¢	$	$$	$$$	$$$$
RESTAURANTS				
under $10	$10–$15	$15–$20	$20–$30	over $30
HOTELS				
under $80	$80–$100	$100–$140	$140–$220	over $220

Restaurant prices are per person for a median main course at dinner. Hotel prices are for a standard double room in season, excluding 6% states sales tax, 1.5% county sales tax, and 5% tourist/bed tax.

BAHIA HONDA KEY

MM 38–36.

All of Bahia Honda Key is devoted to its eponymous state park, which keeps it in a pristine state. Besides the park's outdoor activities, it offers an up-close look of the original railroad bridge.

GETTING HERE AND AROUND

Bahia Honda Key lies a short distance from the southern terminus of the Seven Mile Bridge. A two-lane road travels its 2-mi length. It is 32 mi north of Key West. If you fly into Key West International Airport, you can either rent a car or take the Keys Transit bus to get here.

ESSENTIALS

Transportation Contacts **City of Key West Department of Transportation Key West Transit** (☎ *305/809–3910* ⊕ *www.keywestcity.com*).

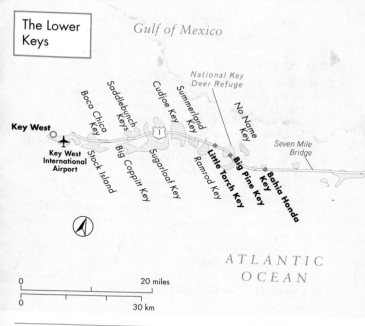

The Lower Keys

Gulf of Mexico

National Key Deer Refuge

Boca Chica Key

Saddlebunch Keys

Cudjoe Key

Summerland Key

No Name Key

Key West

Key West International Airport

Stock Island

Big Coppitt Key

Sugarloaf Key

Ramrod Key

Little Torch Key

Big Pine Key

Bahia Honda

Seven Mile Bridge

ATLANTIC OCEAN

0		20 miles

0		30 km

EXPLORING

★ **Fodor'sChoice** **Bahia Honda State Park.** Most first-time visitors to the region are dismayed by the lack of beaches—but then they discover sun-soaked Bahia Honda Key. The 524-acre park here sprawls across both sides of the highway, giving it 2½ mi of fabulous sandy coastline. The snorkeling isn't bad, either; there's underwater life (soft coral, queen conchs, random little fish) just a few hundred feet offshore. Although swimming, kayaking, fishing, and boating are the main reasons to visit, you shouldn't miss biking along the 2.5 mi of flat roads or walking the 0.25-mile Silver Palm Trail, with rare West Indian plants and several species found nowhere else in the nation. Along the way you'll be treated to a variety of butterflies. Many of the seasonal ranger-led nature programs take place at or depart from the Sand and Sea Nature Center. There are rental cabins, a campground, snack bar, gift shop, 19-slip marina, nature center, and facilities for renting kayaks and arranging snorkeling tours. Get a panoramic view of the island from what's left of the railroad—the Bahia Honda Bridge. ☒ *36850 Overseas Hwy. (MM 37 OS)* ☎ *305/872–2353* ⊕ *www.floridastateparks.*

org/bahiahonda 🖼️*$4.50 for 1 person, $9 for 2 people, 50¢ per additional person* ☉ *Daily 8–sunset.*

WHERE TO STAY

$$$ 🖼️**Bahia Honda State Park.** Elsewhere you'd pay big bucks
★ for the wonderful water views available at these cabins on
Florida Bay. Each of the three cabins has two 2-bedroom
units with a full kitchen and bath and air-conditioning (but
no television, radio, or phone). The park also has popular
campsites ($43 per night) suitable for either tents or motor
homes. Some are directly on the beach—talk about a room
with a view! Cabins and campsites book up early, so reserve
up to 11 months before your planned visit. **Pros:** great bay-
front views; beachfront. **Cons:** books up fast; area can be
buggy. ⊠ *36850 Overseas Hwy. (MM 37 OS)* ☎*305/872–
2353 or 800/326–3521* ⊕*www.reserveamerica.com* ⤳*80
partial hookup campsites, 6 cabin units* ♿*In-room: a/c, no
phone, kitchen, no TV. In-hotel: beachfront, water sports,
bicycles, dump station* ⊟*AE, D, MC, V.*

SPORTS AND THE OUTDOORS

BEACHES

Bahia Honda State Park contains three beaches in all—on
both the Atlantic Ocean and the Gulf of Mexico. Sandspur
Beach, the largest, is regularly declared the best beach in
Florida, and you'll be hard pressed to argue. The sand is
baby-powder soft, and the aqua water is warm, clear, and
shallow. With their mild currents, the beaches are great for
swimming, even with small fry. ⊠ *36850 Overseas Hwy.
(MM 37 OS)* ☎*305/872–2353* ⊕*www.floridastateparks.
org/bahiahonda* 🖼️*$4.50 for 1 person, $9 for 2 people,
50¢ per additional person* ☉ *Daily 8–sunset.*

SCUBA DIVING AND SNORKELING

Bahia Honda Dive Shop (⊠*36850 Overseas Hwy. [MM 37 OS]*
☎*305/872–3210* ⊕*www.bahiahondapark.com*), the con-
cessionaire at Bahia Honda State Park, manages a 19-slip
marina; rents wet suits, snorkel equipment, and corrective
masks; and operates twice-a-day offshore-reef snorkel trips
($30 plus $9 for equipment). Park visitors looking for other
fun can rent kayaks ($12 per hour for a single, $18 for a
double) and beach chairs.

BIG PINE KEY

MM 32–30.

Welcome to the Keys' most natural holdout, where wildlife refuges protect rare and endangered animals. Here you have left behind the commercialism of the Upper Keys for an authentic backcountry atmosphere. How could things get more casual than Key Largo, you might wonder? Find out by exiting U.S. 1 to explore the habitat of the charmingly diminutive Key deer or cast a line from No Name Bridge. Tours explore the expansive waters of National Key Deer Refuge and Great White Heron National Wildlife Refuge, one of the first such refuges in the country. Along with Key West National Wildlife Refuge, it encompasses more than 200,000 acres of water and more than 8,000 acres of land on 49 small islands. Besides its namesake bird, the Great White Heron National Wildlife Refuge provides habitat for uncounted species of birds and three species of sea turtles. It is the only U.S. breeding site for the endangered hawksbill turtle.

GETTING HERE AND AROUND

Most people rent a car to get to Big Pine Key so they can also explore Key West and other parts of the chain.

ESSENTIALS

Visitor Information **Big Pine and the Lower Keys Chamber of Commerce** (✉ 31020 Overseas Hwy. [MM 31 OS], Big Pine Key ☎ 305/872–2411 or 800/872–3722 ⊕ www.lowerkeyschamber.com).

EXPLORING

★ **National Key Deer Refuge.** This 84,351-acre refuge was established in 1957 to protect the dwindling population of the Key deer, one of more than 20 animals and plants classified as endangered or threatened in the Florida Keys. The Key deer, which stands about 30 inches at the shoulders and is a subspecies of the Virginia white-tailed deer, once roamed throughout the Lower and Middle Keys, but hunting, destruction of their habitat, and a growing human population caused their numbers to decline to 27 by 1957. The deer have made a comeback, increasing their numbers to approximately 750. The best place to see Key deer in the refuge is at the end of Key Deer Boulevard and on No Name Key, a sparsely populated island just east of Big Pine Key. Mornings and evenings are the best time to spot them. Deer may turn up along the road at any time of day, so drive slowly. They wander into nearby yards to nibble tender grass and bougainvillea blossoms, but locals do not appreciate tourists driving into their neighborhoods after them. Feeding them is against the law and puts them in danger. The refuge also has 21 other listed endangered and threatened species of plants and animals, including five that are found nowhere else.

Blue Hole. A quarry left over from railroad days, the Blue Hole is the largest body of fresh water in the Keys. From the observation platform and nearby walking trail, you might see the resident alligator (its mate died recently from ingesting a plastic toy), turtles, and other wildlife. There are two well-marked trails: the Jack Watson Nature Trail (0.6 mi), named after an environmentalist and the refuge's first warden; and the Fred Mannillo Nature Trail, one of the most wheelchair-accessible places to see an unspoiled pine-rockland forest and wetlands. The visitor center has exhibits on Keys biology and ecology. The refuge also provides information on the Key West National Wildlife Refuge and the Great White Heron National Wildlife Refuge. Accessible only by water, both are popular with kayak outfitters. ⊠ *Visitor Center–Headquarters, Big Pine Shopping Center (MM 30.5 BS), 179 Key Deer Blvd.* ☎ *305/872–2239* ⊕ *www.fws.gov/nationalkeydeer* ⊒ *Free* ☉ *Daily sunrise–sunset; headquarters weekdays 8–5.*

WHERE TO EAT AND STAY

¢ ✕ **Good Food Conspiracy.** *Vegetarian.* Like good wine, this small natural-foods eatery and market surrenders its pleasures a little at a time. Step inside to the aroma of brewing coffee, and then pick up the scent of fresh strawberries or carrots blending into a smoothie, the green aroma of wheatgrass juice, followed by the earthy smell of hummus. Order raw or cooked vegetarian, vegan, and gluten-free dishes, organic soups and salads, and organic coffees and teas. Bountiful sandwiches (available halved) include the popular tuna melt or hummus and avocado. If you can't sit down for a bite, stock up on healthful snacks like dried fruits, raw nuts, and carob-covered almonds. Dine early: the shop closes at 7 PM Monday to Saturday, and at 5 PM on Sunday. ⊠ *30150 Overseas Hwy. (MM 30.2 OS)* ☎ *305/872–3945* ⊟ *AE, D, MC, V.*

$ ✕ **No Name Pub.** *American.* This no-frills honky-tonk has
★ been around since 1936, delighting inveterate locals and intrepid vacationers who come for the excellent pizza, cold

beer, and *interesting* companionship. The decor, such as it is, amounts to the autographed dollar bills that cover every inch of the place. The full menu printed on place mats includes a tasty conch chowder, a half-pound fried-grouper sandwich, spaghetti and meatballs, and seafood baskets. The lighting is poor, the furnishings are rough, and the music is oldies. This former brothel and bait shop is just before the No Name Key Bridge. It's a bit hard to find, but worth the trouble if you want a singular Keys experience. ⊠*MM 30 BS, turn west on Wilder Rd., left on South St., right on Avenue B, right on Watson Blvd.* ☎*305/872–9115* ⊕*www.nonamepub.com* ⊟*D, MC, V.*

$ ☒**Big Pine Key Fishing Lodge.** There's a congenial atmosphere
★ at this lively family-owned lodge-campground-marina. It's a happy mix of tent campers (who have the fabulous waterfront real estate), RVers (who look pretty permanent), and motel-dwellers who like to mingle at the rooftop pool and challenge each other to a game of poker. Rooms have tile floors, wicker furniture, and doors that allow sea breezes to waft through. A skywalk joins the upper-story rooms with the pool and deck. Campsites range from rustic to full hookups. Everything is spotless—even the campground's bathhouse—and the service is good-natured and efficient. The staff will book you a room, sell you bait, or hook you up with a fishing charter. There are plenty of family-oriented activities, so the youngsters will never complain about being bored. Campsites range between $49 and $57 per night; motel rooms start at $109. Discounts are available for weeklong or longer stays. **Pros:** local fishing crowd; nice pool; great price. **Cons:** RV park is too close to motel; deer will most likely eat your food if you're camping. ⊠*33000 Overseas Hwy. (MM 33 OS)* ☎*305/872–2351* ⛵*16 rooms; 158 campsites, 97 with full hookups, 61 without hookups* ⛵*In-room: a/c (some), no phone, kitchen (some), refrigerator. In-hotel: pool, laundry facilities, Internet terminal, Wi-Fi hotspot* ⊟*D, MC, V.*

$$$$ ☒**Deer Run Bed & Breakfast.** Key deer wander the grounds
★ of this beachfront B&B set on a quiet street lined with buttonwoods and mangroves. Innkeepers Jen DeMaria and Harry Appel were way ahead of the green-lodging game when they opened in 2004. They continue to make strides in environmental- and guest-friendliness, and were recognized as one of the most sustainable inns in the United States by *Islands* magazine in 2009. Two large oceanfront rooms are decorated in soothing earth tones and furnished with mahogany and pecan-wood furnishings. The beach-

4

level unit is decorated in key lime and flamingo-pink, with wicker furnishings, and the garden-view room is an eclectic mix that includes Victorian farmhouse doors serving as the headboard of the queen-size bed. Guests share a living room and a veranda. The mostly organic breakfast menu is suitable for vegans. Guest rooms are stocked with organic cotton towels and cruelty-free toiletries. **Pros:** quiet location; healthy breakfasts; complimentary bike and kayak use. **Cons:** price is a bit high; hard to find. ✉ *1997 Long Beach Dr. (MM 33 OS)* ☎ *305/872–2015* ⊕ *www.deerrunfloridabb.com* ⇆ *4 rooms* ♻ *In-room: a/c, no phone, refrigerator, Wi-Fi. In-hotel: pool, beachfront, water sports, bicycles, no kids under 18* ⊟ *D, MC, V* ⟡ *BP.*

SPORTS AND THE OUTDOORS

BIKING

A good 10 mi of paved roads run from MM 30.3 BS, along Wilder Road, across the bridge to No Name Key, and along Key Deer Boulevard into the National Key Deer Refuge. Along the way you might see some Key deer. Stay off the trails that lead into wetlands, where fat tires can do damage to the environment.

Marty Baird, owner of **Big Pine Bicycle Center** (✉ *31 County Rd. [MM 30.9 BS]* ☎ *305/872–0130*), is an avid cyclist and enjoys sharing his knowledge of great places to ride. He's also skilled at selecting the right bike for the journey, and he knows his repairs, too. His old-fashioned single-speed, fat-tire cruisers rent for $8 per half day and $10 for a full day. Helmets, baskets, and locks are included. Although the shop is officially closed on Sunday, join Marty there most Sunday mornings at 8 from December to Easter for a free off-road fun ride.

FISHING

Cast from No Name Key Bridge or hire a charter to take you into backcountry or deep waters for fishing year-round.

Fish with pros year-round in air-conditioned comfort with **Strike Zone Charters** (✉ *29675 Overseas Hwy. [MM 29.6 BS]*, ☎ *305/872–9863 or 800/654–9560*). Deep-sea charter rates are $600 for a half day, $750 for a full day. Strike Zone also offers flats fishing in the Gulf of Mexico.

KAYAKING

There's nothing like the vast expanse of pristine waters and mangrove islands preserved by national refuges from here to Key West. The mazelike terrain can be confusing, so it's wise to hire a guide at least the first time out.

★ **Big Pine Kayak Adventures** (⊠ *Old Wooden Bridge Fishing Camp [MM 30 BS], turn right at traffic light, continue on Wilder Rd. toward No Name Key* ☎ *305/872–7474* ⊕ *www. keyskayaktours.com*) makes it very convenient to rent kayaks by delivering them to your lodging or anywhere between Seven Mile Bridge and Stock Island. The company, headed by *The Florida Keys Paddling Guide* author Bill Keogh, will rent you a kayak and then ferry you—called taxi-yakking—to remote islands with clear instructions on how to paddle back on your own. Rentals are by the half day or full day. Group kayak tours ($50 for three hours) explore the mangrove forests of Great White Heron and Key Deer National Wildlife Refuges. Custom tours ($125 and up, four hours) transport you to exquisite backcountry areas teeming with wildlife. Kayak fishing charters are also popular.

SCUBA DIVING AND SNORKELING

Close to Looe Key Reef, this is prime scuba and snorkeling territory. Some resorts cater to divers with dive boats that depart from their own dock. Others can make arrangements for you.

Strike Zone Charters (⊠ *29675 Overseas Hwy. [MM 29.5 BS]* ☎ *305/872–9863 or 800/654–9560*) leads dive excursions to the wreck of the 110-foot *Adolphus Busch* ($55), and scuba ($45) and snorkel ($35) trips to Looe Key Reef aboard glass-bottom boats. Strike Zone also offers a five-hour island excursion that combines snorkeling, fishing, and an island cookout for $55 per person. A large dive shop is on-site.

LITTLE TORCH KEY

MM 29–10.

Little Torch Key and its neighbor islands, Ramrod Key and Summerland Key, are good jumping-off points for divers headed for Looe Key Reef. The islands also serve as a refuge for those who want to make forays into Key West but not stay in the thick of things.

The undeveloped backcountry at your door makes Little Torch Key an ideal location for fishing and kayaking. Nearby **Ramrod Key**, which also caters to divers bound for Looe Key, derives its name from a ship that wrecked on nearby reefs in the early 1800s.

NEED A BREAK? The aroma of rich roasting coffee beans at **Baby's Coffee** (✉ 3178 Overseas Hwy. [MM 15 OS], Saddlebunch Keys ☎ 305/744–9866 or 800/523–2326 ⊕ www.babyscoffee.com) arrests you at the door of "the Southernmost Coffee Roaster." Buy it by the pound or by the cup along with fresh baked goods.

WHERE TO EAT

$ ✕ **Geiger Key Marina Smokehouse.** *American.* There's a strong ★ hint of the Old Keys at this ocean-side marina tiki restaurant, on the backside of paradise, as the sign says. Locals usually outnumber tourists; they come for the daily dinner specials, like the BBQ garlic shrimp, smoked sausage with red beans and rice, or buttonwood-smoked chicken. For lunch, try the fresh catch or fried lobster BLT. Weekends are the most popular; the place is packed on Saturday for steak-on-the-grill night and on Sunday for the chicken and ribs barbecue. In season, local fishermen stop here for breakfast before heading out in search of the big ones. ✉ *Geiger Key at 5 Geiger Key Rd., off Boca Chica Rd. (MM 10.7 OS)* ☎ *305/296–3553 or 305/294–1230* ⊕ *www. geigerkeymarina.com* ▭ *D, MC, V* ⊘ *Closed Mon.–Fri. for breakfast Apr.–Dec.*

$$$$ ✕ **Little Palm Island Restaurant.** *Eclectic.* The oceanfront set- ★ ting calls to mind St. Barts and other high-end Caribbean destinations. Keep that in mind as you reach for the bill, which can also make you swoon. The restaurant at the exclusive Little Palm Island Resort—its dining room and adjacent outdoor terrace lit by candles and warmed by live music—is one of the most romantic spots in the Keys. The daily-changing menu melds French and Caribbean flavors, with exotic little touches. Think shrimp and yellowtail ceviche or coconut lobster bisque as a starter, followed by mahimahi with mojo and Creole aioli. The Saturday and Sunday brunch buffet, the full-moon dinners with live entertainment, and Chef's Table Dinner are very popular. The dining room is open to nonguests on a reservations-only basis. ✉ *28500 Overseas Hwy. (MM 28.5 OS)* ☎ *305/872–2551* ⊕ *www.littlepalmisland.com* ⌲ *Reservations essential* ▭ *AE, D, DC, MC, V.*

$$ ✕**Mangrove Mama's Restaurant.** *Seafood.* This could be the prototype for a Keys restaurant, given its shanty appearance, lattice trim, and roving sort of indoor-outdoor floor plan. Then there's the seafood, from the ubiquitous fish sandwich (fried, grilled, broiled, or blackened) to lobster tail, crab cakes, and coconut shrimp. Burgers, steaks, and ribs round out the menu. Hidden in a grove of banana and palm trees, the place opens for lunch and dinner. ✉ *Sugarloaf Key (MM 20 BS)* ☎ *305/745–3030* ▬ *AE, MC, V* ☺ *Closed Sept.*

$$$ ✕**Square Grouper.** *Contemporary.* Although this restaurant's food draws raves, its name earns snickers. (A "square grouper" is slang for bales of marijuana dropped into the ocean during the drug-running 1970s.) Owner Lynn Bell gives the dishes whimsical touches, making them look as good as they taste. The seared sesame-encrusted tuna is lightly crunchy outside, like butter inside. The square grouper sandwich is a steaming pan-sautéed fillet served with key-lime tartar sauce on a ciabatta roll. In an unassuming strip mall, the dining room is surprisingly suave, with linen-swathed tables and a wood-topped zinc bar. ✉ *Cudjoe Key (MM 22.5 OS)* ☎ *305/745–8880* ⊕ *www.squaregrouperbarandgrill.com* ▬ *AE, MC, V* ☺ *Closed Mon. year-round and also Sun. in off-season; closed Sept. and several wks in summer.*

$$ ✕**Sugar Loaf Lodge Restaurant.** *American.* If you're feeling peckish as you drive between Big Pine Key and Key West, there aren't a whole lot of choices. But here's a good place to stop for any meal, especially breakfast. A glass wall lets you admire the Gulf from your table. Dinner, served outside, features Italian dishes like chicken saltimbocca and seafood Alfredo. The chef gives a nod to what's local: snapper with key lime pepper glaze, for instance. ✉ *17015 Overseas Hwy., Sugarloaf Key (MM 17 BS)* ☎ *305/745–3741 or 800/553–6097* ▬ *AE, D, MC, V.*

WHERE TO STAY

★ Fodor'sChoice ☆ **Little Palm Island Resort & Spa.** *Haute tropicale* best describes this luxury retreat, and "second mortgage" might explain how some can afford the extravagant prices. But for those who can, it's worth the price. This property sits on a 5-acre palm-fringed island 3 mi offshore from Little Torch Key. The 28 oceanfront thatch-roof bungalow suites have slate-tile baths, mosquito netting–draped king-size beds, and British colonial–style furnishings. Other comforts include indoor and outdoor showers, a private

$$$$

veranda and separate living room, and fuzzy robes and slippers. Two Island Grand Suites are twice the size of the others and offer his-and-hers bathrooms, an outdoor hot tub, and uncompromising ocean views. To preserve the quiet atmosphere, cell phones are highly discouraged in public areas. **Pros:** secluded setting; heavenly spa; easy wildlife viewing. **Cons:** expensive; might be too quiet for some; low lighting in rooms. ⊠ *28500 Overseas Hwy. (MM 28.5 OS)* ☎ *305/872–2524 or 800/343–8567* ⊕ *www.little-palmisland.com* ⬐ *30 suites* ⬙ *In-room: a/c, no phone, safe, refrigerator, no TV, Internet. In-hotel: restaurant, room service, bars, pool, gym, spa, beachfront, diving, water sports, Wi-Fi hotspot, parking (free), no kids under 16* ⊟ *AE, D, DC, MC, V* ⊚ *MAP.*

$–$$ ⊡ **Looe Key Reef Resort & Center.** If your Keys vacation is all about diving, you'll be well served at this scuba-obsessed operation. The lodging closest to the stellar reef and affordable to boot, it's popular with the bottom-time crowd. Rooms are basic but perfect for sleeping between dives and hanging out at the tiki bar. The one suite is equipped with a fridge and microwave. Single rooms are available. **Pros:** guests get discounts on dive and snorkel trips; fun bar. **Cons:** small rooms; unheated pool; close to road. ⊠ *27340 Overseas Hwy. (MM 27.5 OS), Ramrod Key* ☎ *305/872–2215 Ext. 2 or 800/942–5397* ⊕ *www.diveflakeys.com* ⬐ *23 rooms, 1 suite* ⬙ *In-room: a/c, Wi-Fi. In-hotel: bar, pool, Wi-Fi hotspot* ⊟ *D, MC, V.*

$$–$$$ ⊡ **Parmer's Resort.** Almost every room at this budget-friendly option has a view of South Pine Channel, with the lovely curl of Big Pine Key in the foreground. Waterfront cottages, with decks or balconies, are spread out on six landscaped acres, with a heated swimming pool and a five-hole putting green. There are water sports galore, and the staff will book you a kayak tour, a fishing trip, or a bike excursion, or tell you which local restaurants will deliver dinner to your room. So what if the decor feels a little like Grandma's house and you have to pay extra ($10) if you want your room cleaned daily? **Pros:** bright rooms; pretty setting; good value. **Cons:** a bit out of the way; housekeeping costs extra; little shade around the pool. ⊠ *565 Barry Ave. (MM 28.7 BS)* ☎ *305/872–2157* ⊕ *www.parmersresort.com* ⬐ *18 rooms, 12 efficiencies, 15 apartments, 1 penthouse* ⬙ *In-room: a/c, no phone, kitchen (some). In-hotel: pool, laundry facilities, Wi-Fi hotspot* ⊟ *AE, D, MC, V* ⊚ *CP.*

SPORTS AND THE OUTDOORS

BOATING

Dolphin Marina (✉ *28530 Overseas Hwy., Little Torch Key* ☎ *305/872–2685* ⊕ *www.dolphinmarina.net*) rents 22-foot boats with 150 horsepower for up to eight people by the half day ($219) and full day ($269).

SCUBA DIVING AND SNORKELING

This is the closest you can get on land to Looe Key Reef, and that's where local dive operators love to head.

★ Today **Looe Key Reef** (✉ *216 Ann St. [MM 27.5 OS], Key West* ☎ *305/292–0311*) owes its name to the ill-fated ship. The 5.3-square-nautical-mi reef, part of the **Florida Keys National Marine Sanctuary,** has stands of elkhorn coral on its eastern margin, purple sea fans, and abundant sponges and sea urchins. On its seaward side, it drops almost vertically 50 to 90 feet. In its midst, **Shipwreck Trail** plots the location of nine historic wreck sites in 14 to 120 feet of water. Buoys mark the sites, and underwater signs tell the history of each site and what marine life to expect. Snorkelers and divers will find the sanctuary a quiet place to observe reef life—except in July, when the annual Underwater Music Festival pays homage to Looe Key's beauty and promotes reef awareness with six hours of music broadcast via underwater speakers. Dive shops, charters, and private boats transport about 500 divers and snorkelers to hear the concert, which includes classical, jazz, New Age, and Caribbean music, as well as a little Jimmy Buffett. There are even underwater Elvis impersonators. Rather than the customary morning and afternoon two-tank, two-location trips offered by most dive shops, **Looe Key Reef Resort & Dive Center** (✉ *Looe Key Reef Resort, 27340 Overseas Hwy. [MM 27.5 OS], Ramrod Key* ☎ *305/872–2215 or 877/816–3483* ⊕ *www.diveflakeys.com*), the closest dive shop to Looe Key Reef, runs a single three-tank, three-location dive ($80 for divers, $40 for snorkelers, plus $4 fuel surcharge). The maximum depth is 30 feet, so snorkelers and divers go on the same boat. On Wednesday it runs a dive-only trip that visits the wreck and reefs in the area ($80). The dive boat, a 45-foot catamaran, is docked at the full-service Looe Key Reef Resort.

TOURS

Fantasy Dan's Airplane Rides (✉ *Sugarloaf Key Airport [MM 17], Sugarloaf Key* ☎ *305/304–1214* ⊕ *www.floridaairplanetours.com*) depart from Sugarloaf Key Airport; passengers can spot sharks, sting rays, and other reef life on sightseeing rides priced at $50 per person (sunset and champagne flights are available by special arrangement).

WATER SPORTS

Rent a paddle-propelled vehicle for exploring local Gulf waters at **Sugarloaf Marina** (✉ *17015 Overseas Hwy. [MM 17 BS], Sugarloaf Key* ☎ *305/745–3135*). Rates for a one- or two-person kayak start at $20 for one hour to $40 for a full day. Half days are $30. Delivery is free for multiple-day rentals.

For a guided kayak tour, join Captain Andrea Paulson of **Reelax Charters** (✉ *17015 Overseas Hwy. [MM 17 BS] at Sugarloaf Marina, Sugarloaf Key* ☎ *305/304–1392* ⊕ *www.keyskayaking.com*). Customized charters start at four hours for $60 per person and can include snorkeling and beaching on a secluded island in the Keys backcountry.

Key West

WORD OF MOUTH

"While I do agree that Key West can be a bit risqué at times, it is a place where families can go and have a great family vacation."

—cgenster

"Whether Key West is 'worth it' depends on what kind of vacation towns you like. Do you like funky, lively, outdoor eating, lots of young people in the streets, lots of open bars with loud music, and a Caribbean flavor? If so, you might like Key West. I do."

—montereybob

Updated
by Chelle
Koster
Walton

SITUATED 150 MI FROM MIAMI, 90 mi from Havana, and an immeasurable distance from sanity, this end-of-the-line community has never been like anywhere else. Even after it was connected to the rest of the country—by the railroad in 1912 and by the highway in 1938—it maintained a strong sense of detachment. The U.S. acquired Key West from Spain in 1821, along with the rest of Florida. The Spanish had named the island Cayo Hueso, or Bone Key, after the Native American skeletons they found on its shores. In 1823 President James Monroe sent Commodore David S. Porter to chase pirates away. For three decades the primary industry in Key West was wrecking—rescuing people and salvaging cargo from ships that foundered on the nearby reefs. According to some reports, when pickings were lean the wreckers hung out lights to lure ships aground. Their business declined after 1849, when the federal government began building lighthouses.

In 1845 the army began construction on Fort Taylor, which kept Key West on the Union side during the Civil War. After the fighting ended, an influx of Cubans unhappy with Spain's rule brought the cigar industry here. Fishing, shrimping, and sponge gathering became important industries, as did pineapple canning. Through much of the 19th century and into the 20th, Key West was Florida's wealthiest city in per-capita terms. But in 1929 the local economy began to unravel. Cigar making moved to Tampa, Hawaii dominated the pineapple industry, and the sponges succumbed to blight. Then the Depression hit, and within a few years half the population was on relief.

Tourism began to revive Key West, but that came to a halt when a hurricane knocked out the railroad bridge in 1935. To help the tourism industry recover from that crushing blow, the government offered incentives for islanders to turn their charming homes—many of them built by shipwrights—into guesthouses and inns. The wise foresight has left the town with more than 100 such lodgings, a hallmark of Key West vacationing today. In the 1950s the discovery of "pink gold" in the Dry Tortugas boosted the economy of the entire region. Catching Key West shrimp required a fleet of up to 500 boats and flooded local restaurants with some of the sweetest shrimp alive. The town's artistic community found inspiration in the colorful fishing boats.

Key West reflects a diverse population: Conchs (natives, many of whom trace their ancestry to the Bahamas), freshwater Conchs (longtime residents who migrated from somewhere else years ago), Hispanics (primarily Cuban immigrants), recent refugees from the urban sprawl of mainland Florida, military personnel, and an assortment of vagabonds, drifters, and dropouts in search of refuge. The island was once a gay vacation hot spot, and it remains a decidedly gay-friendly destination. Some of the once-renowned gay guesthouses, however, no longer cater to an exclusively gay clientele. Key Westers pride themselves on their tolerance of all peoples, all sexual orientations, and even all animals. Most restaurants allow pets, and it's not surprising to see stray cats, dogs, and even chickens roaming freely through the dining rooms. The chicken issue is one that government officials periodically try to bring to an end, but the colorful fowl continue to strut and crow, particularly in the vicinity of Old Town's Bahamian Village.

Although the rest of the Keys are known for outdoor activities, Key West has something of a city feel. Few open spaces remain, as promoters continue to churn out restaurants, galleries, shops, and museums to interpret the city's intriguing past. As a tourist destination, Key West has a lot to sell—an average temperature of 79°F, 19th-century architecture, and a laid-back lifestyle. Yet much has been lost to those eager for a buck. Duval Street looks like a miniature Las Vegas, lined with garish signs for T-shirt shops and tour-company offices. Cruise ships dwarf the town's skyline and fill the streets with day-trippers gawking at the hippies with dogs in their bike baskets, gay couples walking down the street holding hands, and the oddball lot of locals, some of whom bark louder than the dogs.

ORIENTATION AND PLANNING

PLANNING

GETTING HERE AND AROUND

Between mile markers 4 and 0, Key West is the one place in the Keys where you could conceivably do without a car, especially if you plan on staying around Old Town. If you've driven the 106 mi down the chain, you're probably ready to abandon your car in the hotel parking lot anyway. Trolleys, buses, bikes, scooters, and feet are more suitable alternatives. When your feet tire, catch a rickshaw-style pedicab ride, which will run you about $1.50 a minute. To explore the beaches, New Town, and Stock Island, you'll probably need a car.

Greyhound Lines runs a special Keys shuttle two times a day (depending on the day of the week) from Miami International Airport (departing from Concourse E, lower level) and stops throughout the Keys. Fares run about $39 for Key West (3535 S. Roosevelt, Key West International Airport). Keys Shuttle runs scheduled service six times a day in 15-passenger vans between Miami Airport and Key West with stops throughout the Keys for $70 to $90 per person. Key West Express operates air-conditioned ferries between the Key West Terminal (Caroline and Grinnell streets) and Miami, Marco Island, and Fort Myers Beach. The trip from Fort Myers Beach takes at least four hours each way and costs $85.50 one way, $145 round-trip. Ferries depart from Fort Myers Beach at 8:30 AM and from Key West at 6 PM. The Miami and Marco Island ferry costs $85.50 one way and $119 round-trip, and departs at 8:30 AM. A photo ID is required for each passenger. Advance reservations are recommended. The SuperShuttle charges $102 per passenger for trips from Miami International Airport to the Upper Keys. To go farther into the Keys, you must book an entire 11-person van, which costs about $350 to Key West. You need to place your request for transportation back to the airport 24 hours in advance.

The City of Key West Department of Transportation has eight color-coded bus routes traversing the island from 5:30 AM to 11:30 PM. Stops have signs with the international bus symbol. Schedules are available on buses and at hotels, visitor centers, and shops, and online. The fare is $2 one way. Its Lower Keys Shuttle bus runs between Marathon to Key West ($3 one way), with scheduled stops along the way.

ESSENTIALS

Transportation Contacts **City of Key West Department of Transportation Key West Transit** (☎ 305/809–3910 ⊕ www.keywestcity. com). **Greyhound Lines** (☎ 800/410–5397 or 800/231–2222). **Keys Shuttle** (☎ 305/289–9997 or 888/765–9997 ⊕ www.floridakeysshuttle.com). **Key West Express** (✉ 100 Grinnell St. ☎ 888/539–2628 ⊕ www.seakeywestexpress.com). **Lower Keys Shuttle** (☎ 305/809–3910 ⊕ www.monroecounty-fl.gov). **SuperShuttle** (☎ 305/871–2000 ⊕ www.supershuttle.com). **Florida Keys Taxi Dispatch** (☎ 305/296–6666 or 305/296–1800 ⊕ www.keywesttaxi.com). **Luxury Limousine** (☎ 305/367–2329 or 800/664–0124).

TOP REASONS TO GO

■ **The Dry Tortugas.** Do a day trip to Dry Tortugas National Park for snorkeling and hiking away from the throngs.

■ **Watching the Sunset.** Revel in both the beautiful sunset and the gutsy performers at Mallory Square's nightly celebration.

■ **The Conch Train.** Hop aboard the Conch Train for a narrated tour of the town's tawdry past and rare architectural treasures.

■ **Bar-Hopping.** Nightlife rules in Key West. Do the "Duval Crawl," the local version of club-hopping. But first fortify yourself at one of the town's exceptional restaurants.

■ **The Hemingway Connection.** Visit Ernest Hemingway's historic home for a page out of Key West's literary past.

5

Visitor Information Greater Key West Chamber of Commerce (⊠ 510 Greene St. ☎ 305/294–2587 or 800/527–8539 ⊕ www.key-westchamber.org). **Gay and Lesbian Community Center of Key West** (⊠ 513 Truman Ave., Key West ☎ 305/292–3223 ⊕ www.glcckeywest.org). **Key West Business Guild (gay)** (⊠ 513 Truman Ave. ⛫ Box 1208, Key West ☎ 305/294–4603 ⊕ www.gaykeywestfl.com).

RESTAURANTS

Keys restaurants get their most exotic once you reach Key West, and you can pretty much find anything you want (although bargains are hard to come by). Pricier restaurants serve tantalizing fusion cuisine that reflects the influence of Cuba and other Caribbean islands. Tropical fruits and citrus figure prominently on the menus, and mango, papaya, and passion fruit show up on the lists of beverages. Of course, there are plenty of places that serve local seafood. Key West stays true to island character with a selection of "hole-in-the-wall" places where it doesn't get any more colorful.

HOTELS

Key West's lodgings include historic cottages, restored Conch houses, and large resorts. Quaint guesthouses, the town's trademark, offer a true island experience in residential neighborhoods near Old Town's restaurants, shops, and clubs. A few rooms cost as little as $65 a night in the off-season, but most range from $100 to $300. Some guesthouses and inns do not welcome children under 16, and most do not permit smoking.

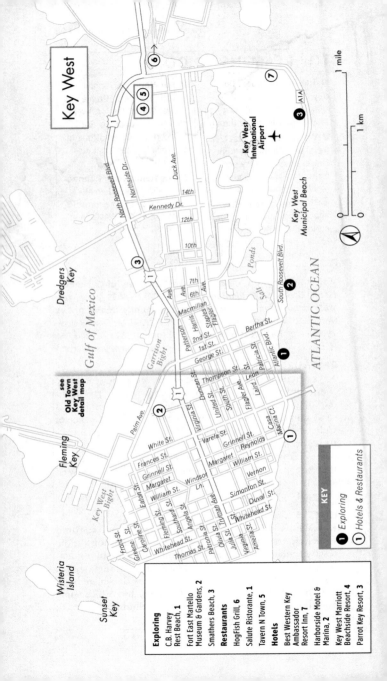

Key West

KEY

① Exploring

① Hotels & Restaurants

Exploring

C.B. Harvey
Rest Beach, 1

Fort East Martello
Museum & Gardens, 2

Smathers Beach, 3

Restaurants

HogFish Grill, 6

Salute Ristorante, 1

Tavern N Town, 5

Hotels

Best Western Key
Ambassador
Resort Inn, 7

Harborside Motel &
Marina, 2

Key West Marriott
Beachside Resort, 4

Parrot Key Resort, 3

Gulf of Mexico

Wisteria Island

Sunset Key

Fleming Key

Dredgers Key

Key West Bight

Garrison Bight

see
Old Town
Key West
detail map

Palm Ave.

White St.

Frances St.

Grinnell St.

Margaret

William St.

Windsor Ln.

Eaton St.

Fleming St.

Southard St.

Angela St.

Caroline St.

Whitehead St.

Greene St.

Front St.

Thomas St.

Petronia St.

Olivia St.

Truman Ave.

Julia St.

Virginia St.

Amelia St.

Simonton St.

Duval St.

Whitehead St.

Vernon

Reynolds

William St.

Margaret

Grinnell St.

Varela St.

United St.

South St.

Thompson St.

Duncan St.

Virginia St.

Laird

Flagler Ave.

Leon

Patricia St.

Atlantic Blvd.

Casa Marina Ct.

George St.

1st St.

2nd St.

Patterson

Harris

Staples Ave.

Flagler

Macmillan

6th Ave.

7th Ave.

Bertha St.

Salt Ponds

South Roosevelt Blvd.

North Roosevelt Blvd.

10th

12th

14th

Kennedy Dr.

Duck Ave.

Northside Dr.

Key West International Airport

Key West Municipal Beach

A1A

ATLANTIC OCEAN

1 mile

1 km

N

WHAT IT COSTS				
¢	$	$$	$$$	$$$$
RESTAURANTS				
under $10	$10–$15	$15–$20	$20–$30	over $30
HOTELS				
under $80	$80–$100	$100–$140	$140–$220	over $220

Restaurant prices are per person for a main course at dinner. Hotel prices are for a standard double room in season, excluding 6% state sales tax, 1.5% county sales tax, and 5% tourist/bed tax.

OLD TOWN

5

The heart of Key West, the historic Old Town area runs from White Street to the waterfront. Beginning in 1822, wharves, warehouses, chandleries, ship-repair facilities, and eventually in 1891 the U.S. Custom House sprang up around the deep harbor to accommodate the navy's large ships and other sailing vessels. Wreckers, merchants, and sea captains built lavish houses near the bustling waterfront. A remarkable number of these fine Victorian and pre-Victorian structures have been restored to their original grandeur, and now serve as homes, guesthouses, shops, restaurants, and museums. These, along with the dwellings of famous writers, artists, and politicians who've come to Key West over the past 175 years, are among the area's approximately 3,000 historic structures. Old Town also has the city's finest restaurants and hotels, lively street life, and popular nightspots.

TIMING

Allow two full days to see all the Old Town museums and homes, especially with a little shopping thrown in. For a narrated trip on the tour train or trolley, budget an hour to ride the loop without getting off, an entire day if you plan to get off and on at some of the sights and restaurants.

A GOOD TOUR

To cover many sights, take the Old Town Trolley, which lets you get off and reboard a later trolley, or the Conch Tour Train. Old Town is also manageable on foot, bicycle, moped, or electric cars. The area is expansive, so you'll want either to pick and choose from the stops on this tour or break it into two or more days. Start on Whitehead Street at the **Ernest Hemingway Home & Museum**, then cross the street and climb to the top of the **Lighthouse Museum** for a spectacular view. Return to Whitehead Street and follow it north to Angela Street, where you'll turn right. At Margaret Street, the **City Cemetery** is worth a look for its above-ground vaults and unusual headstone inscriptions. Head north on Margaret Street, turn left onto Southard Street, then right onto Simonton Street. Halfway up the block, **Nancy Forrester's Secret Garden** occupies Free School Lane. After wandering among the blossoms, return again to Southard Street, turn right, and follow it through Truman Annex to **Fort Zachary Taylor State Park**.

Walk west into Truman Annex to see the **Harry S. Truman Little White House Museum**, President Truman's vacation residence. Return east on Caroline and turn left on Whitehead to visit the **Audubon House and Gardens**, honoring the famed artist and naturalist. Follow Whitehead north to Greene Street and turn left to see the salvaged sea treasures of the **Mel Fisher Maritime Heritage Society Museum**. At Whitehead's northern end are the **Key West Aquarium** and the **Key West Museum of Art and History**, the former historic U.S. Custom House. By late afternoon you should be ready to cool off with a dip or catch a few rays at the beach. From the aquarium, head east two blocks to the end of Simonton Street, where you'll find the appropriately named **Simonton Street Beach**. Like all Key West beaches, it is man-made, with white sand imported from the Bahamas and north Florida. If you've brought your pet, stroll a few blocks east to **Dog Beach**, at the corner of Vernon and Waddell streets. A little farther east is **Higgs Beach–Astro Park**, on Atlantic Boulevard between White and Reynolds streets. As the sun starts to sink, return to the north end of Old Town and follow the crowds to Mallory Square, behind the aquarium, to watch Key West's nightly sunset spectacle. For dinner, head east on Caroline Street to **Historic Seaport at Key West Bight**.

EXPLORING

TOP ATTRACTIONS

④ Audubon House and Tropical Gardens. If you've ever seen an engraving by ornithologist John James Audubon, you'll understand why his name is synonymous with birds. See some of his original works portraying local birds in this three-story house, which was built in the 1840s for Captain John Geiger and is filled with period furniture similar to what Geiger salvaged off shipwrecks. The home now commemorates Audubon's 1832 stop in Key West while he was traveling through Florida to study birds. Docents lead a guided tour ($7.50) that points out the rare orchids and other plants and trees in the garden. An art gallery sells lithographs of the artist's famed portraits. ⊠ *205 Whitehead St.* ☎ *305/294–2116 or 877/294–2470* ⊕ *www.audubonhouse.com* ☞ *$12* ⊙ *Daily 9:30–5, last tour starts at 4:15.*

① Ernest Hemingway Home and Museum. Amusing anecdotes
★ spice up the guided tours of Ernest Hemingway's home, built in 1801 by the town's most successful wrecker. While living here between 1931 and 1942, Hemingway wrote about 70% of his life's work, including classics like *For Whom the Bell Tolls.* Few of his belongings remain aside from some books, and there's little about his actual work, but photographs help you visualize his day-to-day life. The supposed six-toed descendants of Hemingway's cats—many named for actors, artists, authors, and even a hurricane—have free rein of the property. Tours begin every 15 minutes and take 25–30 minutes; then you're free to explore on your own. ⊠ *907 Whitehead St.* ☎ *305/294–1136* ⊕ *www. hemingwayhome.com* ☞ *$12* ⊙ *Daily 9–5.*

NEED A BREAK? Check out the pretty palm garden next to the Key West Library at 700 Fleming Street, just off Duval. This leafy, outdoor reading area, with shaded benches, is the perfect place to escape the frenzy and crowds of downtown Key West. There's free Internet access in the library, too.

㉑ Fort Zachary Taylor Historic State Park. Construction of the
★ fort began in 1845 but halted during the Civil War. Even though Florida seceded from the Union, Yankee forces used the fort as a base to block Confederate shipping. More than 1,500 Confederate vessels were detained in Key West's harbor. The fort, finally completed in 1866, was also used in the Spanish-American War. Take a 30-minute guided walking tour of the fort, a National Historic Land-

5

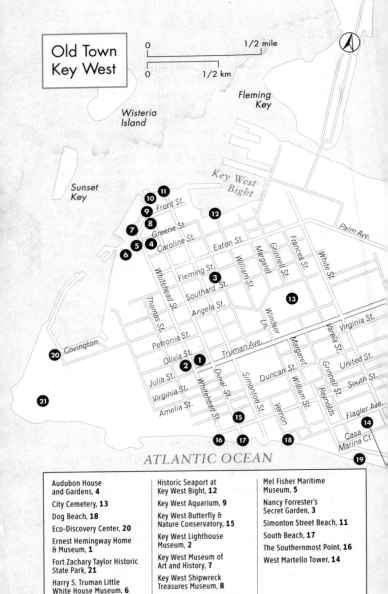

Old Town Key West

0 — 1/2 mile
0 — 1/2 km

Fleming Key

Wisteria Island

Sunset Key

Key West Bight

Front St.

Greene St.

Caroline St.

Eaton St.

Fleming St.

Southard St.

Angela St.

Petronia St.

Olivia St.

Julia St.

Virginia St.

Amelia St.

Whitehead St.

Thomas St.

Margaret St.

William St.

Frances St.

Grinnell St.

White St.

Palm Ave.

Windsor Ln.

Truman Ave.

Duncan St.

Simonton St.

Duval St.

Whitehead St.

Vernon

Margaret St.

William St.

Virginia St.

United St.

South St.

Varela St.

Grinnell St.

Reynolds

Flagler Ave.

Casa Marina Ct.

Covington

ATLANTIC OCEAN

Audubon House and Gardens, 4

City Cemetery, 13

Dog Beach, 18

Eco-Discovery Center, 20

Ernest Hemingway Home & Museum, 1

Fort Zachary Taylor Historic State Park, 21

Harry S. Truman Little White House Museum, 6

Higgs Beach-Astro City Playground, 19

Historic Seaport at Key West Bight, 12

Key West Aquarium, 9

Key West Butterfly & Nature Conservatory, 15

Key West Lighthouse Museum, 2

Key West Museum of Art and History, 7

Key West Shipwreck Treasures Museum, 8

Mallory Square & Pier, 10

Mel Fisher Maritime Museum, 5

Nancy Forrester's Secret Garden, 3

Simonton Street Beach, 11

South Beach, 17

The Southernmost Point, 16

West Martello Tower, 14

GAY AND PROUD

With its official motto being "One Human Family," Key West has long been a favorite of the gay and lesbian community. In fact, Key West wouldn't be the same without the gay people who renovated many of the ramshackle homes and guesthouses. Following are a couple of the gay-specific activities Key West offers.

Home of the Key West Business Guild, the **Gay & Lesbian Community Center** (✉ 513 Truman Ave. ☎ 305/292–3223 or 800/535–7797 ⊕ www. gaykeywestfl.com) hosts events, movie nights, and support groups. Stop at the visitor center for information on gay accommodations and attractions. It's open daily 9 to 5.

Decorated with a rainbow, the **Gay & Lesbian Trolley Tour** (✉ 513 Truman Ave. ☎ 305/294–4603 ⊕ www. gaykeywestfl.com) rumbles around the town beginning at 11 every Saturday morning. The 70-minute tour highlighting Key West's gay history costs $25.

The name says it all. **Skinny Dipper Cruises** (✉ Garrison Bight Marina ☎ 305/240–0517 ⊕ www.skinny-dippercruises.com) offers clothing-optional excursions. Sunset sails are $75 per person, while longer charter cruises are $125 per person.

mark, at noon and 2, or self-tour the redbrick structure anytime between 8 and 5. In February a celebration called Civil War Heritage Days includes costumed reenactments and demonstrations. From mid-January to mid-April the park serves as an open-air gallery for pieces created for Sculpture Key West. One of its most popular features is its man-made beach, a rest stop for migrating birds in the spring and fall; there are also hiking and biking trails and a kayak launch. ✉ Box 6565; end of Southard St., through Truman Annex ☎ 305/292–6713 ⊕ www.floridastateparks. org/forttaylor ☞ $4.50 for 1 person, $7 for 2 people, 50¢ per additional person ($2.50 for pedestrians and cyclists) ☉ Daily 8–sunset, tours noon and 2.

❻ Harry S. Truman Little White House Museum. Recent renova-
★ tions to this circa-1890 landmark have restored the home and gardens to the Truman era, down to the wallpaper pattern. A free photographic review of visiting dignitaries and presidents—John F. Kennedy, Jimmy Carter, and Bill Clinton are among the chief executives who passed through

here—is on display in the back of the gift shop. Engaging 45-minute tours begin every 20 minutes until 4:30. They start with an excellent 10-minute video on the history of the property and Truman's visits. On the grounds of **Truman Annex,** a 103-acre former military parade grounds and barracks, the home served as a winter White House for presidents Truman, Eisenhower, and Kennedy. Note: the tour does require climbing steps. Visitors can do a free self-guided botanical tour of the grounds with a free brochure from the museum store. ⊠ *111 Front St.* ☎ *305/294–9911* ⊕ *www.trumanlittlewhitehouse.com* 🖃 *$15* ⊙ *Daily 9–5, grounds sunrise–6; last tour at 4:30.*

⑲ Higgs Beach–Astro City Playground. This Monroe County park ☮ with its groomed pebbly sand is a popular sunbathing spot. A nearby grove of Australian pines provides shade, and an Italian restaurant provides shelter should a storm suddenly sweep in. Kayak and beach-chair rentals are available, as is a volleyball net. The beach also has a marker and cultural exhibit commemorating the gravesite of 295 enslaved Africans who died after being rescued from three South America–bound slave ships in 1860. Across the street, **Astro City Playground** is popular with young children. ⊠ *Atlantic Blvd. between White and Reynolds Sts.* ☎ *No phone* 🖃 *Free* ⊙ *Daily 6 AM–11 PM.*

⑫ Historic Seaport at Key West Bight. What used to be a funky—in some places even seedy—part of town is now an 8½-acre historic restoration project of 100 businesses, including waterfront restaurants, open-air bars, museums, clothing stores, bait shops, dive shops, docks, a marina, water sports, and concessions. It's all linked by the 2-mi waterfront **Harborwalk,** which runs between Front and Grinnell streets, passing tall ships, schooners, sunset cruises, fishing charters, and glass-bottom boats. ⊠ *100 Grinnell St.* ☎ *305/293–8309.*

NEED A BREAK? Get your morning (or afternoon) buzz at **Coffee Plantation** (⊠ *713 Caroline St.* ☎ *305/295–9808* ⊕ *www.coffee-plantationkeywest.com*), where you can also hook up to the Internet in the comfort of a homelike setting in a circa-1890 Conch house. Munch pastries or sandwiches and wraps and sip a hot or cold espresso beverage.

⑮ Key West Butterfly & Nature Conservatory. This air-conditioned ★ refuge for butterflies, birds, and the human spirit gladdens ☮ the soul with hundreds of colorful wings—some 40 spe-

Hemingway Was Here

In a town where Pulitzer Prize–winning writers are almost as common as coconuts, Ernest Hemingway stands out. Bars and restaurants around the island claim that he ate or drank there.

Hemingway came to Key West in 1928 at the urging of writer John dos Passos, and rented a house with wife number two, Pauline Pfeiffer. They spent winters in the Keys and summers in Europe and Wyoming, occasionally taking African safaris. Along the way they had two sons, Patrick and Gregory. In 1931 Pauline's wealthy uncle Gus gave the couple the house at 907 Whitehead Street. Now known as the Ernest Hemingway Home & Museum, it's Key West's number-one tourist attraction. Renovations included the addition of a pool and a tropical garden.

In 1935, when the visitor bureau included the house in a tourist brochure, Hemingway promptly built the brick wall that surrounds it today. He wrote of the visitor bureau's offense in a 1935 essay for *Esquire,* saying, "The house at present occupied by your correspondent is listed as number eighteen in a compilation of the forty-eight things for a tourist to see in Key West. So there will be no difficulty in a tourist finding it or any other of the sights of the city, a map has been prepared by the local F.E.R.A. authorities to be presented to each arriving visitor. This is all very flattering to the easily bloated ego of your correspondent but very hard on production."

During his time in Key West, Hemingway penned some of his most important works, including *A Farewell to Arms, To Have and Have Not, Green Hills of Africa,* and *Death in the Afternoon.* His rigorous schedule consisted of writing almost every morning in his second-story studio above the pool, then promptly descending the stairs at midday. By afternoon and evening he was ready for drinking, fishing, swimming, boxing, and hanging around with the boys.

One close friend was Joe Russell, a craggy fisherman and owner of the rugged bar Sloppy Joe's, originally at 428 Greene Street but now at 201 Duval Street. Russell was the only one in town who would cash Hemingway's $1,000 royalty check. Russell and Charles Thompson introduced Hemingway to deep-sea fishing, which became fodder for his writing.

Hemingway stayed in Key West for 11 years before leaving Pauline for wife number three. Pauline and the boys stayed on in the house, which sold in 1951 for $80,000, 10 times its original cost.

—Jim and Cynthia Tunstall

cies of butterflies alone—in a lovely glass-encased bubble. Waterfalls, artistic benches, paved pathways, birds, and lush, flowering vegetation elevate this above most butterfly attractions. The gift shop and gallery are worth a visit on their own. ⊠ *1316 Duval St.* ☎ *305/296–2988* ⊕ *www. keywestbutterfly.com* ⊿ *$12* ☉ *Daily 9–5 (last admission 4:30); gallery and shop open until 5:30.*

★ FodorsChoice **Key West Museum of Art & History in the Custom**
❼ **House.** Key West was designated a U.S. port of entry in the early 1820s, and a customs house was established by 1891. Salvaged cargoes from ships wrecked on the reefs were brought here, setting the stage for Key West's becoming for a time the richest city in Florida. The imposing redbrick-and–terra-cotta Richardsonian Romanesque–style building reopened as a museum and art gallery in 1999 after $9 million worth of restoration work. Galleries have long-term and changing exhibits about national artists, the history of Key West (including a Hemingway room with running video), and a fine collection of folk artist Mario Sanchez's wood paintings. In 2011, to commemorate the 100th anniversary of the railroad's arrival to Key West in 1912, a new Flagler exhibit opened. ⊠ *281 Front St.* ☎ *305/295–6616* ⊕ *www.kwahs.com* ⊿ *$10* ☉ *Daily 9:30-4:30.*

❷ **Key West Lighthouse Museum & Keeper's Quarters Museum.** For the best view in town, climb the 88 steps to the top of this 1847 lighthouse. The 92-foot structure has a Fresnel lens, which was installed in the 1860s at a cost of $1 million. The keeper lived in the adjacent 1887 clapboard house, which now exhibits vintage photographs, ship models, nautical charts, and lighthouse artifacts from all along the Key reefs. A kids' room is stocked with books and toys. ⊠ *938 Whitehead St.* ☎ *305/295–6616* ⊕ *www.kwahs.com* ⊿ *$10* ☉ *Daily 9:30–5; last admission at 4:30.*

❿ **Mallory Square and Pier.** For most cruise-ship passengers this is the disembarkation point for an attack on Key West. For practically every visitor, it's the requisite venue for a nightly sunset celebration that includes street performers—human statues, sword swallowers, tightrope walkers, musicians, and more—plus craft vendors, conch fritter fryers, and other regulars who defy classification. (Want a picture with my pet iguana?) With all the activity, don't forget to watch the main show: a dazzling tropical sunset. ⊠ *Mallory Sq.* ☎ *No phone.*

16 **The Southernmost Point.** Possibly the most photographed site in Key West (even though the actual geographic southernmost point in the continental United States lies across the bay on a naval base, where you see a satellite dish), this is a must-see for many visitors. Who wouldn't want a picture taken next to the big striped buoy that marks the spot? A plaque next to it honors Cubans who lost their lives trying to escape to America, and other signs tell Key West history. ⊠ *Whitehead and South Sts.* ☎ *No phone.*

WORTH NOTING

13 **City Cemetery.** You can learn almost as much about a town's history through its cemetery as through its historic houses. Key West's celebrated 20-acre burial place may leave you wanting more, with headstone epitaphs such as "I told you I was sick," and, for a wayward husband, "Now I know where he's sleeping at night." Among the interesting plots are a memorial to the sailors killed in the sinking of the battleship USS *Maine,* carved angels and lambs marking graves of children, and grand aboveground crypts that put to shame many of the town's dwellings for the living. There are separate plots for Catholics, Jews, and refugees from Cuba. You're free to walk around the cemetery on your own, but the best way to see it is on a 60-minute tour given by the staff and volunteers of the Historic Florida Keys Foundation. Tours leave from the main gate, and reservations are required. ⊠ *Margaret and Angela Sts.* ☎ *305/292–6718* ⊕ *www.historicfloridakeys.org* ⊠ *Tours $15* ☉ *Daily sunrise–6 PM, tours Tues. and Thurs. at 9:30 year-round; call for additional times.*

18 **Dog Beach.** Next to Louie's Backyard, this tiny beach—the only one in Key West where dogs are allowed unleashed—has a shore that's a mix of sand and rocks. ⊠ *Vernon and Waddell Sts.* ☎ *No phone* ⊠ *Free* ☉ *Daily sunrise–sunset.*

20 **Eco-Discovery Center.** While visiting Fort Zachary Taylor Historic State Park, stop in at this 6,400-square-foot interactive attraction, which encourages visitors to venture through a variety of Florida Keys habitats, from pinelands, beach dunes, and mangroves to the deep sea. Walk through a model of NOAA's (National Oceanic and Atmospheric Administration) Aquarius, a unique underwater ocean laboratory 9 mi off Key Largo, to virtually discover what lurks beneath the sea. Touch-screen computer displays, a dramatic movie, a 2,450-gallon aquarium, and live underwater cameras show off North America's only contiguous barrier coral reef. ⊠ *35 E. Quay Rd., at end of Southard St. in Truman Annex* ☎ *305/809–4750* ⊕ *floridakeys.noaa.gov* 🖃 *Free, donations accepted* ⊙ *Tues.–Sat. 9–4.*

❾ **Key West Aquarium.** Pet a nurse shark's tail and explore the fascinating underwater realm of the Keys without getting wet at this historic aquarium. Hundreds of tropical fish and fascinating sea creatures live here. A touch tank enables you to handle starfish, sea cucumbers, and horseshoe and hermit crabs. You can see queen conchs—living totems of the Conch Republic—in one of the no-touch tanks. Built in 1934 by the Works Progress Administration as the world's first open-air aquarium, most of the building has been enclosed for all-weather viewing. Guided tours, included in the admission price, feature shark, sting ray, and sea turtle feedings. ⊠ *1 Whitehead St.* ☎ *305/296–2051* ⊕ *www.keywestaquarium.com* 🖃 *$12* ⊙ *Daily 10–6; tours at 11, 1, 3, and 4:30.*

❽ **Key West Shipwreck Treasures Museum.** Much of Key West's history, early prosperity, and interesting architecture come from ships that ran aground on its coral reef. Artifacts from the circa-1856 *Isaac Allerton*, which yielded $150,000 worth of wreckage, comprise the museum portion of this multifaceted attraction. Actors and films add a bit of Disneyesque drama. The final highlight is climbing to the top the 65-foot lookout tower, a reproduction of the 20 or so towers used by Key West wreckers during the town's salvaging heyday. ⊠ *1 Whitehead St.* ☎ *305/292–8990* ⊕ *www.shipwreckhistoreum.com* 🖃 *$12* ⊙ *Daily 9:40–5.*

❺ **Mel Fisher Maritime Museum.** In 1622 two Spanish galleons laden with riches from South America foundered in a hurricane 40 mi west of the Keys. In 1985 diver Mel Fisher recovered the treasures from the lost ships, the *Nuestra Señora de Atocha* and the *Santa Margarita*. Fisher's incredible adventure tracking these fabled hoards and battling the State of Florida for rights is as amazing as the loot you'll see, touch, and learn about in this museum. Artifacts include a circa-1620 78-carat natural emerald crystal worth almost $250,000. Exhibits on the second floor rotate, and might cover slave ships, including the excavated 17th-century *Henrietta Marie*, or silver booty recovered from the sea. ⊠ *200 Greene St.* ☎ *305/294–2633* ⊕ *www.melfisher.org* 🖃 *$12* ⊙ *Weekdays 8:30–6, weekends 9:30–6 (last tickets sold at 5:15).*

❸ Nancy Forrester's Secret Garden. It's hard to believe that this green escape still exists in the middle of Old Town Key West. Despite damage by hurricanes and pressures from developers, Nancy Forrester has maintained her naturalized garden for more than 40 years. Growing in harmony are rare palms and cycads, ferns, bromeliads, bright gingers and heliconias, gumbo-limbo trees strewn with orchids and vines, and a colorful crew of parrots, cats, and a few surprises. An art gallery has botanical prints and environmental art. One-hour private tours cost $35 per person, four-person minimum. ⊠ *1 Free School La.* ☎ *305/294-0015* ⊕ *www.nancyforrester.com* ☑ *$10 self-tour* ⊙ *Daily 10–5.*

⓫ Simonton Street Beach. This small beach facing the gulf is a great place to watch boat traffic in the harbor. Parking, however, is difficult. There are restrooms and a boat ramp. ⊠ *North end of Simonton St.* ☎ *No phone* ☑ *Free* ⊙ *Daily 7 AM–11 PM.*

⓱ South Beach. On the Atlantic, this stretch of sand, also known as City Beach, is popular with travelers staying at nearby motels. It is now part of the new Southernmost Hotel on the Beach resort, but is open to the public with a fun beach bar and grill. There's no parking, however, so visitors must walk or bike to the beach. ⊠ *Foot of Duval St.* ☎ *No phone* ☑ *Free* ⊙ *Daily 7 AM–11 PM.*

⓮ West Martello Tower. Among the arches and ruins of this Civil War–era fort, the Key West Garden Club maintains lovely gardens of native and tropical plants, fountains, and sculptures overlooking the beach. It also holds art, orchid, and flower shows February through April and in November, and leads private garden tours one weekend in March. ⊠ *Atlantic Blvd. and White St.* ☎ *305/294-3210* ⊕ *www. keywestgardenclub.com* ☑ *Donation welcome* ⊙ *Tues.– Sat. 9:30–3:15.*

ALWAYS CELEBRATING. Key West has a growing calendar of festivals and artistic and cultural events—including the Conch Republic Celebration in April and the Halloween Fantasy Fest in October. December brings festivity in the form of a lighted boat parade at the Historic Seaport and New Year's Eve revelry that rivals any in the nation. Few cities of its size—a mere 2 mi by 4 mi—celebrate with the joie de vivre of this one.

NEW TOWN

The Overseas Highway splits as it enters Key West, the two forks rejoining to encircle New Town, the area east of White Street to Cow Key Channel. The southern fork runs along the shore as South Roosevelt Boulevard (Route A1A) and skirts Key West International Airport. Part of New Town was created with dredged fill. The island would have continued growing this way had the Army Corps of Engineers not determined in the early 1970s that it was detrimental to the nearby reef.

TIMING

Allow one to two hours to include brief stops at each attraction. If your interests lie in art, gardens, or Civil War history, you'll need three or four hours. Throw in time at the beach and make it a half-day affair.

A GOOD TOUR. Attractions are few in New Town. The best way to take in the sights is by car or motor scooter. Take South Roosevelt Boulevard from the island's entrance to the historical museum exhibits at **East Martello Tower**, near the airport. Continue past the salt ponds and stop at **Smathers Beach** for a dip, or continue west onto Atlantic Boulevard to **C.B. Harvey Rest Beach**. Between it and Higgs Beach, visit the lovely gardens at **West Martello Tower**.

EXPLORING

❶ **C.B. Harvey Rest Beach.** This beach and park were named after Cornelius Bradford Harvey, former Key West mayor and commissioner. It has half a dozen picnic areas, dunes, and a wheelchair and bike path. ⊠ *Atlantic Blvd., east side of White St. Pier* ☎ *No phone* ⊠ *Free* ⊙ *Daily 7* AM–11 PM.

❷ **Fort East Martello Museum & Gardens.** This redbrick Civil
★ War fort never saw a lick of action during the war. Today it serves as a museum, with historical exhibits about the 19th and 20th centuries. Among the latter are relics of the USS *Maine*, cigar factory and shipwrecking exhibits, and the citadel tower you can climb to the top. The museum, operated by the Key West Art and Historical Society, also has a collection of Stanley Papio's "junk art" sculptures inside and out, and a gallery of Cuban folk artist Mario Sanchez's chiseled and painted wooden carvings of historic Key West street scenes. ⊠ *3501 S. Roosevelt Blvd.*

THE CONCH REPUBLIC

Beginning in the 1970s, pot smuggling became a source of income for islanders who knew how to dodge detection in the maze of waterways in the Keys. In 1982 the U.S. Border Patrol threw a roadblock across the Overseas Highway just south of Florida City to catch drug runners and undocumented aliens. Traffic backed up for miles as Border Patrol agents searched vehicles and demanded that the occupants prove U.S. citizenship. Officials in Key West, outraged at being treated like foreigners by the federal government, staged a protest and formed their own "nation," the so-called Conch Republic. They hoisted a flag and distributed mock border passes, visas, and Conch currency. The embarrassed Border Patrol dismantled its roadblock, and now an annual festival recalls the city's victory.

☎ *305/296–3913* ⊕*www.kwahs.com* ☎*$6* ⊙ *Weekdays 10–4, weekends 9:30–4:30.*

❸ **Smathers Beach.** This wide beach has nearly 2 mi of sand,
★ plus restrooms, picnic areas, and volleyball courts, all of
☾ which make it popular with the spring-break crowd. Trucks along the road rent rafts, Windsurfers, and other beach "toys." Metered parking is on the street. ✉ *S. Roosevelt Blvd.* ☎*No phone* ☎*Free* ⊙ *Daily 7* AM*–11* PM.

WHERE TO EAT

Bring your appetite, a sense of daring, and a lack of preconceived notions about propriety. A meal in Key West can mean overlooking the crazies along Duval Street, watching roosters and pigeons battle for a scrap of food that may have escaped your fork, relishing the finest in what used to be the dining room of some 19th-century Victorian home, or gazing out at boats jockeying for position in the marina. And that's just the diversity of the setting. Seafood dominates local menus, but the treatment afforded that fish or crustacean can range from Cuban and New World to Asian and continental.

$$–$$$ ✕**Ambrosia.** *Japanese.* Ask any savvy local where to get the best sushi on the island, and you'll undoubtedly be pointed to this tiny wood-and-tatami-paneled dining room with indoor waterfall tucked away in a resort near the beach.

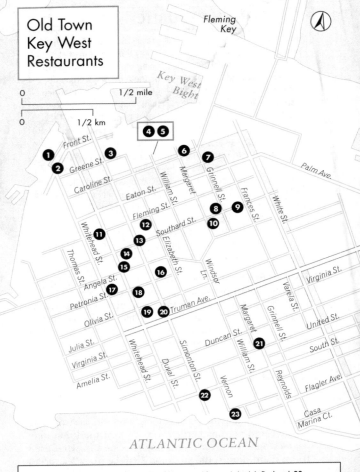

Old Town Key West Restaurants

Fleming Key

Key West Bight

Front St.

Greene St.

Caroline St.

Eaton St.

William St.

Margaret

Grinnell St.

Frances St.

White St.

Palm Ave.

Fleming St.

Southard St.

Elizabeth St.

Whitehead St.

Thomas St.

Angela St.

Petronia St.

Olivia St.

Julia St.

Virginia St.

Amelia St.

Windsor Ln.

Virginia St.

Varela St.

Grinnell St.

United St.

South St.

Margaret

William St.

Duncan St.

Truman Ave.

Whitehead St.

Duval St.

Simonton St.

Vernon

Reynolds

Flagler Ave.

Casa Marina Ct.

ATLANTIC OCEAN

0   1/2 mile

0   1/2 km

Ambrosia, 22
Bistro 245, 2
Blue Heaven, 17
B. O.'s Fish Wagon, 6
The Cafe, A Mostly
Vegetarian Place, 14
Café Marquesa, 12
Café Solé, 9
Conch Republic Seafood
Company, 3

Croissants de France, 18
El Meson de Pepe's, 1
El Siboney, 21
Finnegan's Wake Irish Pub
and Eatery, 7
Half Shell Raw Bar, 5
Jimmy Buffett's
Margaritaville Cafe, 11
Lobo's Mixed Grill, 15

Louie's Backyard, 23
Mangia Mangia, 8
Michael's Restaurant, 10
Nine One Five, 19
Pisces, 20
SaraBeth's, 13
Seven Fish, 16
Turtle Kraals, 4

Grab a seat at the sushi bar and watch owner and head sushi chef Masa prepare an impressive array of superfresh sashimi delicacies. Sushi lovers can't go wrong with the Ambrosia special ($35), a sampler of five kinds of sashimi, seven pieces of sushi, and sushi rolls. There's an assortment of lightly fried tempura and teriyaki dishes and a killer bento box at lunch. Enjoy it all with a glass of premium sake or a cold glass of Sapporo beer. ⊠ *Santa Maria Resort, 1401 Simonton St.* ☎ *305/293–0304* ⊕ *www.keywestambrosia. com* ▭ *AE, D, MC, V* ⊘ *No lunch weekends. Closed 2 weeks after Labor Day.*

$ ✕**B.O.'s Fish Wagon.** *Seafood.* What started out as a fish
★ house on wheels appears to have broken down on the corner of Caroline and William streets and is today the cornerstone for one of Key West's junkyard-chic dining institutions. Step up to the wood-plank counter window and order the specialty: a grouper sandwich fried or grilled and topped with key lime sauce. Other choices include fish nuts (don't be scared, they're just fried nuggets), hot dogs, and shrimp or soft-shell-crab sandwich. Talk sass with your host and find a picnic table or take a seat at the plank. Grab some paper towels off one of the rolls hanging around and busy yourself reading graffiti, license plates, and irreverent signs. It's a must-do Key West experience. ⊠ *801 Caroline St.* ☎ *305/294–9272* ▭ *No credit cards.*

$$$ ✕**Bistro 245.** *Seafood.* The sunset views alone are worth a visit, but the food here is stellar as well. Start upstairs at the bar with a key lime martini and watch the throngs below make Mallory Square a scene. Downstairs, you can choose between the open-air patio or the air-conditioned dining room with picture-window views. For dinner, try the lobster quesadilla or seafood cocktail as an appetizer before moving on to the shrimp and lobster fettuccine with asparagus and chèvre, seared mahi with tangerine butter, or yellowtail snapper with coconut-lemongrass sauce. The breakfast menu features healthy options like fruit smoothies and smoked salmon, tofu, and avocado on a bagel. Creative salads and sandwiches make lunch an intriguing affair. ⊠ *245 Front St., Westin Key West Resort* ☎ *305/294–4000* ⊕ *www.westin.com/keywest* ▭ *AE, D, DC, MC, V.*

$$$ ✕**Blue Heaven.** *Caribbean.* The outdoor dining area here is
★ often referred to as "the quintessential Keys experience," and it's hard to argue. There's much to like about this historic restaurant where Hemingway refereed boxing matches and customers cheered for cockfights. Although these events are no more, the free-roaming chickens and cats add that

"what-a-hoot" factor. Nightly specials include black-bean soup, Provençal sea scallops, jerk chicken, and sautéed yellowtail snapper in citrus beurre blanc. Desserts and breads are baked on the premises; the banana bread, pineapple pancakes, and lobster Benedict with key lime hollandaise are hits during "breakfast with the roosters," the restaurant's signature meal. ⊠ *729 Thomas St.* ☎ *305/296–8666* ⊕ *www.blueheavenkw.com* ⌒ *Reservations not accepted* ▤ *AE, D, MC, V* ⊙ *Closed after Labor Day for 6 weeks.*

$ ✕ **The Cafe, A Mostly Vegetarian Place.** *Vegetarian.* You don't have to be a vegetarian to love this new-age café decorated with bright artwork and a corrugated tin–fronted counter. Local favorites include homemade soup, veggie burgers (order them with a side of sweet-potato fries), grilled portobello mushroom salad, seafood, vegan specialties, and grilled Gorgonzola pizza. For bigger appetites there are offerings like the Szechuan-style vegetable stir-fry. ⊠ *509 Southard St.* ☎ *305/296–5515* ▤ *D, MC, V.*

★ **Fodor's Choice** ✕ **Café Marquesa.** *Continental.* Chef Susan Ferry
$$$ presents seven or more inspired entrées on her changing menu each night; carefully executed dishes can include yellowtail snapper with pear; ricotta pasta purses with caponata and red pepper coulis; and Australian rack of lamb crusted with goat cheese and a port-fig sauce. End your meal on a sweet note with a key lime napoleon with tropical fruits and berries. There's also a fine selection of wines and custom martinis such as the key limetini and the Irish martini. Adjoining the intimate Marquesa Hotel, the dining room is equally relaxed and elegant. ⊠ *600 Fleming St.* ☎ *305/292–1244* ⊕ *www.marquesa.com* ▤ *AE, DC, MC, V* ⊙ *No lunch.*

$$$ ✕ **Café Solé.** *French.* Welcome to the "home of the hog snapper," a deliciously roasted local fish seasoned with a red-pepper-custard sauce. This little piece of France is concealed behind a high wall and a gate in a residential neighborhood. Inside, Chef John Correa marries his French training with local ingredients, creating delicious takes on classics, including portobello mushroom soup, snapper with mango salsa, and some of the best bouillabaisse you'll find outside of Marseilles. From the land, there is filet mignon with a wild-mushroom demi-glace. If you can't decide, a three-course tasting dinner costs $27. Creative salads, carpaccios, and sandwiches star on the lunch menu. ⊠ *1029 Southard St.* ☎ *305/294–0230* ⊕ *www.cafesole.com* ▤ *AE, D, DC, MC, V* ⊙ *Closed Wed.*

$$$ ✕ **Conch Republic Seafood Company.** *Seafood.* Because of its location where the fast ferry docks, Conch Republic does a brisk business. It's huge, open-air, and on the water, so the place is hard to miss. The menu is ambitious, offering more than just standard seafood fare. The baked oysters callaloo (a spinachlike green), for instance, are a Caribbean-style twist on oysters Rockefeller. The grilled or fried shrimp basket comes with a trio of sauces, including the house mixture. Paella, plantain-crusted mahi, seafood stir-fry, and steaks are some other options. Live music adds to the decibel level. ✉ *631 Greene St., at Elizabeth St.* ☎ *305/294–4403* ⊕ *www.conchrepublicseafood.com* ⊟ *AE, D, MC, V.*

$$$ ✕ **Croissants de France.** *French.* Pop into the bakery for something sinfully sweet—a key lime beignet perhaps?—or spend some time people-watching at the sidewalk café next door. Quiche and crepes are the standouts at lunch. The new dinner menu offers a select list of Continental specialties such as chicken cordon bleu and seafood-filled puff pastry. Finish off your meal with a dessert crepe or a chocolate éclair. ✉ *816 Duval St.* ☎ *305/294–2624* ⊕ *www.croissants-defrance.com* ⊟ *AE, D, MC, V* ⊘ *Closed Wed.*

$$ ✕ **El Meson de Pepe.** *Caribbean.* If you want to get a taste of the island's Cuban heritage, this is the place. Perfect for after Mallory Square sunset, you can dine alfresco or in the dining room on refined versions of Cuban classics. Begin with a mega-size mojito while you enjoy the basket of bread and savory sauces. The expansive menu offers *tostones rellenos* (green plantains with different traditional fillings), ceviche (raw fish "cooked" in citrus juice marinade), and more for starters. Choose from Cuban specialties such as roasted pork in a cumin mojo sauce and *ropa vieja* (shredded beef stew). At lunch, the local Cuban population and cruise-ship passengers enjoy Cuban sandwiches and smaller versions of dinner's most popular entrées. A salsa band performs outside at the bar during sunset celebration. ✉ *Mallory Sq., 410 Wall St.* ☎ *305/295–2620* ⊕ *www.elmesondepepe.com* ⊟ *AE, D, MC, V.*

$ ✕ **El Siboney.** *Caribbean.* Dining at this family-style restaurant is like going to Mom's for Sunday dinner—if your mother is Cuban. The dining room is noisy, and the food is traditional *cubano*. There are well-seasoned black beans, a memorable paella, traditional *ropa vieja* (shredded beef and roast pork), and local seafood served grilled, stuffed, and breaded. Dishes come with Cuban bread, salad or plantains, and rice or fries. To make a good thing even better, the prices are very reasonable. In case you're confused by the headdressed Indian images, Siboney is the name of an ancient Caribbean tribe. ⊠ *900 Catherine St.* ☎ *305/296–4184* ⊕ *www.elsiboneyrestaurant.com* ☐ *AE, DC, MC, V.*

$ ✕ **Finnegan's Wake Irish Pub and Eatery.** *Irish.* "Come for the beer—Stay for the food—Leave with the staff" is the slogan of this popular pub. The pictures of Beckett, Shaw, Yeats, and Wilde on the walls and the creaky wood floors underfoot exude Irish country warmth. The certified Angus beef is a bit pricey ($30 for an 18-ounce rib eye), but most of the other dishes are bargains. Traditional fare includes bangers and mash, chicken potpie, and colcannon—rich mashed potatoes with scallions, sauerkraut, and melted white cheddar cheese. Bread pudding soaked with a honey-whiskey sauce is a true treat. Live music on weekends and daily happy hours from 4 to 7 and midnight to 2 featuring nearly 30 beers on tap make it popular with the spring-break and sometimes noisy drinking crowd. ⊠ *320 Grinnell St.* ☎ *305/293–0222* ⊕ *www.keywestirish.com* ☐ *AE, D, MC, V.*

$–$$ ✕ **Half Shell Raw Bar.** *Seafood.* Smack-dab on the docks, this legendary institution gets its name from the oysters, clams, and peel-and-eat shrimp that are a departure point for its seafood-based diet. It's not clever recipes or fine dining (or even air-conditioning in most parts) that packs 'em in; it's fried fish, po'boy sandwiches, and seafood combos. For a break from the deep fryer, try the light and spicy conch ceviche "cooked" with lime juice. The potato salad is flavored with dill, and the "Pama Rita" is a new twist in Margaritaville. ⊠ *Lands End Village at Historic Seaport, 231 Margaret St.* ☎ *305/294–7496* ⊕ *www.halfshellrawbar. com* ☐ *AE, MC, V.*

$ ✕ **Hogfish Bar & Grill.** *Seafood.* It's worth a drive to Stock ★ Island, the next island up from Key West, to sit along one of Florida's last surviving working waterfronts, watch the shrimpers and fishermen unloading their catch, and indulge in the freshness you're witnessing at this down-to-earth spot. Hogfish (catfish) is of course the specialty. The "Killer Hogfish Sandwich" comes on Cuban Bread. Sprinkle it with one of the house hot sauces. Other favorites include lobster BLT or pulled pork sandwiches at lunch and hogfish tacos, gator bites, lobster and shrimp potpie, or smoked ribs at dinner. ⊠ *6810 Front St., Stock Island* ☎ *305/293–4041* ⊕ *www.hogfishbar.com* ☐ *D, MC, V.*

$$ ✕ **Jimmy Buffett's Margaritaville Cafe.** *Southern.* If you must have your cheeseburger in paradise, it may as well be here, where you can chew along with the songs playing on the

sound system. The first of Buffet's line of chain eateries, it belongs here more than anywhere else, but quite frankly it's more about the name, music, and attitude (and margaritas) than the food. The menu has a Cajun-Caribbean flair, with such offerings as conch chowder (good and spicy!), blackened hot dog, grilled andouille sausage with red beans and rice, grilled mahi with pineapple-mango salsa, and barbecued ribs. Live bands pack the place come dinner and into the wee hours. ✉ *500 Duval St.* ☎ *305/292–1435* ⊕ *www.margaritaville.com* ▭ *AE, D, MC, V.*

$$$ ✕ **Latitudes.** *Eclectic.* For a special treat, take the short boat
★ ride to lovely Sunset Key for lunch or dinner on the beach. Creativity and quality ingredients combine for dishes that are bound to impress as much as the setting. For lunch, the fish tacos with chipotle aioli and salsa are a fine example of the chef's use of local foods. At dinner, start with the crispy lobster cakes or seared yellowfin tuna stacked with mango, then move on to one of the delightful entrées, such as yellowtail snapper with roasted tomato broth, sweet potato–crusted grouper, or Wagyu skirt steak with mocha demi-glace. Choose a table inside looking out over the gulf or on the patio. The restaurant also serves breakfast. ✉ *Sunset Village, 245 Front St.* ☎ *305/292–5300 or 888/477–7786* ⊕ *www.sunsetkeyisland.com* ⚓ *Reservations essential* ▭ *AE, D, DC, MC, V.*

¢ ✕ **Lobo's Mixed Grill.** *American.* Juicy burgers and a variety of 30 different roll-up sandwiches (rib eye, oyster, grouper, and others) have earned this tucked-away corner a loyal following. The menu includes salads and quesadillas, as well as a fried shrimp and oyster combo. This courtyard food stand closes at 5, so eat early. Most of Lobo's business is takeout (it has eight outdoor picnic tables), and it offers free delivery within Old Town. ✉ *5 Key Lime Sq., east of intersection of Southard and Duval Sts.* ☎ *305/296–5303* ⊕ *www.loboskeywest.com* ▭ *No credit cards* ☉ *Closed Sun. Apr.–early Dec.*

$$$$ ✕ **Louie's Backyard.** *Eclectic.* Feast your eyes on a steal-your-
★ breath-away view and beautifully presented dishes prepared by executive chef Doug Shook. Once you get over sticker shock on the seasonally changing menu (appetizers cost around \$9–\$18; entrées can hover around the \$37 mark), settle in on the outside deck and enjoy dishes like seared coriander scallops with tangerine sauce, grilled fillet with wild mushrooms and tomato bordelaise, and mustard-crusted chicken breast. A new, more affordable option opened upstairs in late 2009, the Upper Deck, serving tapas

CLOSE UP

Everything's Fishy in the Keys

Fish. It's what's for dinner (and lunch—and sometimes even breakfast!) in the Florida Keys. The Keys' runway between the Gulf of Mexico or Florida Bay and Atlantic warm waters means fish of many fin. Restaurants take full advantage by serving it fresh, whether you caught it or a local fisherman did.

Menus at a number of colorful waterfront shacks such as **Snapper's** (⊠ 139 Seaside Ave., Key Largo ☎ 305/852–5956) in Key Largo and **Half Shell Raw Bar** (⊠ 231 Margaret St., Key West ☎ 305/294–7496) range from basic raw, steamed, broiled, grilled, or blackened fish to some Bahamian and New Orleans–style interpretations. Other seafood houses dress up their tables in linens and their fish in creative haute-cuisine styles, such as **Pierre's** (⊠ MM 81.5 BS, Islamorada ☎ 305/664–3225) hogfish meuniere or sashimi of yellowfin tuna at **Barracuda Grill** (⊠ 4290 Overseas Hwy.,

Marathon ☎ 305/743–3314). And if you're looking for that seafood breakfast Keys-style, try the "grits and grunts"—fried fish and grits—at **The Stuffed Pig** (⊠ 3520 Overseas Hwy., Marathon ☎ 305/743–4059).

You know it's fresh when you see a fish market as soon as you open the door to the restaurant where you're dining. It happens all the time in the Keys. You can even study the seafood showcases and pick the fish fillet or lobster tail you want.

Many of the Keys' best restaurants are found in marina complexes, where the commercial fishermen bring their catches straight from the sea. Some, however, such as **Hogfish Bar & Grill** on Stock Island, one island north of Key West (⊠ 6810 Front St., Stock Island ☎ 305/293–4041 ⊕ www.hogfishbar.com), and **Keys Fisheries Market & Marina** (⊠ End of 35th St., Marathon, MM 49 BS ☎ 305/743–4353 or 866/743–4353), take some finding.

such as flaming ouzo shrimp, roasted olives with onion and feta, and Gruyère and duck confit pizza. If you come for lunch, the menu is less expensive, but the view is just as fantastic. For night owls, the tin-roofed Afterdeck Bar serves cocktails on the water until the wee hours. ⊠ 700 Waddell Ave. ☎ 305/294–1061 ⊕ www.louiesbackyard.com ⌂ Reservations essential ⊟ MC, V ☺ Closed Labor Day to mid-Sept., Upper Deck closed Sun.–Mon.

$$ ✕ **Mangia Mangia.** *Italian.* This longtime favorite serves
★ large portions of homemade pastas that diners can match

with any of the homemade sauces. Tables are arranged in a brick garden hung with twinkling lights and in a cozy, casual dining room in an old house. Everything out of the open kitchen is outstanding, including the *bollito misto di mare* (fresh seafood sautéed with garlic, shallots, white wine, and pasta) or the memorable spaghettini "schmappellini," homemade pasta with asparagus, tomatoes, pine nuts, and Parmesan. The wine list—with more than 350 offerings—includes old and rare vintages, and also has a good by-the-glass selection. ⊠ *900 Southard St.* ☎ *305/294–2469* ⊕ *www.mangia-mangia.com* ▭ *AE, D, MC, V* ⊘ *No lunch*.

$$$ ✕**Michaels Restaurant.** *American.* White tablecloths, subdued lighting, and romantic music give Michaels the feel of an urban eatery. Garden seating reminds you that you are in the Keys. Chef-owner Michael Wilson flies in prime rib, cowboy steaks, and fillets from Allen Brothers in Chicago, which has supplied top-ranked steak houses for more than a century. Also on the menu is a melt-in-your-mouth grouper stuffed with jumbo lump crab, Wagyu meatloaf, veal saltimbocca, and a variety of made-to-order fondue dishes (try the pesto pot, spiked with hot pepper and basil). The Hemingway (mojito-style) and the Third Degree (raspberry vodka and white crème de cacao) top the cocktail menu. ⊠ *532 Margaret St.* ☎ *305/295–1300* ⊕ *www.michaelskeywest.com* ▭ *AE, MC, V* ⊘ *No lunch*.

$$$ ✕**Nine One Five.** *Eclectic.* Twinkling lights draped along the lower- and upper-level outdoor porches of a 100-year-old Victorian mansion set an elegant—though unstuffy—stage at this tapas-style eatery. If you like to sample and sip, you'll appreciate the variety of smaller plate selections and wines by the glass. Taster-portioned tapas include olives, cheese, shrimp, and pâté, or try a combination with the tapas platter or the signature "tuna dome," with fresh crab, lemon-miso dressing, and an ahi tuna–sashimi wrapping. There are also larger plates if you're craving something like seafood soup or steak au poivre frites. Dine outdoors and people-watch along upper Duval, or sit at a table inside while listening to light jazz. ⊠ *915 Duval St.* ☎ *305/296–0669* ⊕ *www.915duval.com* ▭ *AE, MC, V* ⊘ *No lunch*.

$$$$ ✕**Pisces.** *Continental.* In a circa-1892 former store and ★ home, chef William Arnel and staff create a contemporary setting with a stylish granite bar, Andy Warhol originals, and glass oil lamps. On the menu, favorites include "lobster tango mango," flambéed in cognac and served with saffron butter sauce and sliced mangoes. Other dishes include Pisces Aphrodite (seafood in puff pastry), veal chops with

wild mushrooms, and raspberry duck. ✉ *1007 Simonton St.* ☎ *305/294–7100* ⊕ *www.pisceskeywest.com* ▭ *AE, MC, V* ⊘ *No lunch.*

$$ ✕ **Salute Ristorante at the Beach.** *Italian.* This colorful restaurant sits on Higgs Beach, giving it one of the island's best lunch views—and a bit of sand and salt spray on a windy day. Owners of the popular Blue Heaven restaurant recently took it over, and have designed an intriguing dinner menu that includes linguine with mussels, vegetable or three-cheese meat lasagna, and white-bean soup. At lunch, the gazpacho refreshes with great flavor and texture, and the calamari marinara, antipasti sandwich, pasta primavera, and yellowtail sandwich do not disappoint. ✉ *1000 Atlantic Blvd., Higgs Beach* ☎ *305/292–1117* ⊕ *www.saluteonthe-beach.com* ▭ *AE, D, MC, V.*

$$ ✕ **Sarabeth's.** *American.* Named for the award-winning
★ jam-maker and pastry chef Sarabeth Levine, who runs the kitchen, it naturally is proclaimed for its all-morning, all-afternoon breakfast, best enjoyed in the picket-fenced front yard of this sweet circa-1870 cottage. Lemon ricotta pancakes, pumpkin waffles, omelets, and homemade jams make the meal. Lunch offerings range from a griddled smoked mozzarella sandwich to poached salmon "Cobb" sandwich. Start dinner with the signature velvety cream of tomato soup, or roasted red beets and Gorgonzola salad. The daily special augments the eight-entrée listings that include chicken potpie, green chile pepper macaroni with three cheeses, and grilled mahi with tomatillo sauce. In the mood for dessert? The warm orange-apricot bread pudding takes its cues from Sarabeth's most popular flavor of jam. ✉ *530 Simonton St.* ☎ *305/293–8181* ⊕ *www.sarabeths-keywest.com* ▭ *AE, D, MC, V* ⊘ *Closed Mon. and Tues.*

$$$ ✕ **Seven Fish.** *Seafood.* A local hot spot, this off-the-beaten-track eatery is good for an eclectic mix of dishes like tropical shrimp salsa, wild-mushroom quesadilla, seafood marinara, and a mixed grill of chicken, shrimp, and veggies. Those in the know arrive early for dinner to snag one of the 12 or so tables clustered in the bare-bones dining room. ✉ *632 Olivia St.* ☎ *305/296–2777* ⊕ *www.7fish.com* ▭ *AE, D, MC, V* ⊘ *Closed Tues. No lunch.*

$$ ✕ **Tavern N Town.** *Eclectic.* This handsome and warm restaurant has an open kitchen that adds lovely aromas from the wood-fired oven. The menu offers a variety of options such as small plates of shrimp cocktail and Wagyu beef sliders, sharing plates of drunken mussels and paella, and small pizzas for starters. Spanish plancha seafood dishes

seared on polished steel slabs, like the tamarind-glazed shrimp, and wild Scottish salmon, are the restaurant's signature offerings. Breakfast, lunch, and dinner are all served here. ⊠ *Key West Marriott Beachside Resort, 3841 N. Roosevelt Blvd.* ☎ *305/296–8100 or 800/546–0885* ⊕ *www.beachsidekeywest.com* ⌂ *Reservations essential* ⊟ *AE, D, DC, MC, V.*

$$ ✕**Turtle Kraals.** *Seafood.* Named for the kraals, or corrals,
☾ where sea turtles were once kept until they went to the cannery, this place calls to mind the island's history. The menu offers an assortment of marine cuisine that includes seafood enchiladas, mesquite-grilled fish of the day, and mango crab cakes. The newest addition, a slow-cook wood smoker, results in wonderfully tender ribs, brisket, mesquite-grilled oysters with Parmesan and cilantro, and chargrilled chicken. Breakfast offers some interesting and quite tasty options like barbecued hash and eggs or huevos rancheros. The open restaurant overlooks the marina at the Historic Seaport. Turtle races entertain during happy hour on Mondays and Fridays. ⊠ *231 Margaret St.* ☎ *305/294–2640* ⊕ *www.turtlekraals.com* ⊟ *AE, MC, V.*

WHERE TO STAY

Historic cottages, restored century-old Conch houses, and large resorts are among the offerings in Key West, the majority charging between $100 and $300 a night. In high season, December through March, you'll be hard pressed to find a decent room for less than $200, and most places raise prices considerably during holidays and festivals. Many guesthouses and inns do not welcome children under 16, and most do not permit smoking indoors. Most tariffs include an expanded Continental breakfast and, often, afternoon wine or snack.

$$$$ ▦**Ambrosia Key West.** If you desire personal attention, a
★ casual atmosphere, and a dollop of style, stay at these twin inns spread out on nearly 2 acres. Ambrosia is more intimate, with themed rooms such as the Treetop, Sailfish Suites, and Havana Cabana. Ambrosia Too is a delightful art-filled hideaway. Rooms and suites have original work by local artists, wicker or wood furniture, and spacious bathrooms. Each has a private entrance and deck, patio, or porch. Poolside full breakfast is included, and children are welcome. **Pros:** spacious rooms; poolside breakfast; friendly staff. **Cons:** on-street parking can be tough to find;

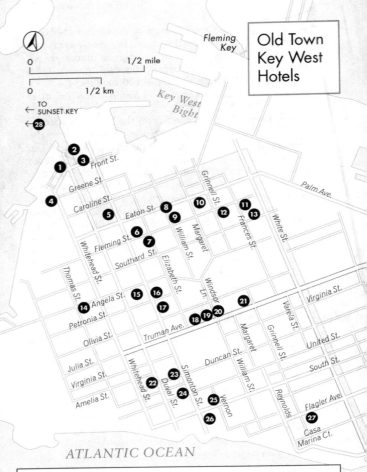

Old Town Key West Hotels

Fleming Key

Key West Bight

Front St.

Greene St.

Caroline St.

Eaton St.

Whitehead St.

Fleming St.

Southard St.

Thomas St.

Angela St.

Petronia St.

Olivia St.

Truman Ave.

Julia St.

Virginia St.

Amelia St.

Duval St.

Simonton St.

Duncan St.

Margaret St.

William St.

Grinnell St.

Varela St.

Virginia St.

United St.

South St.

Reynolds

Flagler Ave.

Casa Marina Ct.

Windsor Ln.

Elizabeth St.

Grinnell St.

Margaret

William St.

Frances St.

White St.

Palm Ave.

Vernon

TO SUNSET KEY

ATLANTIC OCEAN

Ambrosia Key West, **6**

Angelina Guest House, **14**

Azul Key West, **21**

Casa Marina Resort, **27**

Courtney's Place, **16**

Eden House, **12**

The Gardens Hotel, **15**

Heron House Court, **11**

Hyatt Key West Resort & Spa, **3**

Island City House Hotel, **9**

Island House, **13**

Key Lime Inn, **18**

Key West B&B/ Popular House, **8**

La Pensione, **20**

Marquesa Hotel, **7**

Merlin Guesthouse, **17**

Mermaid & the Alligator, **19**

Ocean Breeze Inn, **25**

Ocean Key Resort & Spa, **1**

Pearl's Rainbow, **23**

Pier House Resort & Caribbean Spa, **2**

Reach Resort, **26**

Simonton Court, **5**

Southernmost Hotel , **24**

Speakeasy Inn, **22**

Sunset Key Guest Cottages, **28**

Westin Key West Resort & Marina, **4**

Westwinds Inn, **10**

a little too spread out. ⊠ *622 Fleming St.* ☎ *305/296–9838 or 800/535–9838* ⊕ *www.ambrosiakeywest.com* ⊅ *6 rooms, 3 town houses, 1 cottage, 10 suites* ⚿ *In-room: a/c, kitchen (some), refrigerator, Wi-Fi. In-hotel: pools, bicycles, Wi-Fi hotspot, pets allowed* ⊟ *AE, D, MC, V* ⊚ *BP.*

$$–$$$ 🖾 **Angelina Guest House.** The high rollers and ladies of the night were chased away long ago, but this charming guest-house revels in its past as a gambling hall and bordello. In the heart of Old Town Key West, it's a home away from home that offers simple, clean, attractively priced accom-modations, which range from small rooms sharing a bath to spacious rooms with king beds and sleeper sofas. Built in the 1920s, this yellow-and-blue clapboard building has sec-ond-floor porches, gabled roofs, and a white picket fence. The current owners prettied the rooms with flower-print curtains and linens and added homemade cinnamon rolls, which receive rave reviews. A lagoon-style pool, fountain, and old-brick walkways accent a lovely garden. **Pros:** good value; nice garden; friendly staff. **Cons:** thin walls; basic rooms; shared balcony. ⊠ *302 Angela St.* ☎ *305/294–4480 or 888/303–4480* ⊕ *www.angelinaguesthouse.com* ⊅ *13 rooms* ⚿ *In-room: a/c, no phone, refrigerator (some), no TV, Wi-Fi. In-hotel: pool, no kids under 18, Wi-Fi hotspot* ⊟ *D, MC, V* ⊚ *CP.*

$$$– 🖾 **Azul Key West.** The ultramodern—nearly minimalistic—
$$$$ redo of this classic circa-1903 Queen Anne mansion is a break from the sensory overload of Key West's other abundant Victorian guesthouses. The adults-only boutique hotel, 3½ blocks from Duval Street, combines original trim, high ceilings, and shiny wood floors with sleek furnish-ings, including a curved frosted-glass-and-chrome check-in desk, leather loungers, and a state-of-the-art sound system. Spacious, serene rooms, some with private verandas, have leather headboards, flat-screen TVs, and remote-controlled fans and lights. **Pros:** lovely building; marble-floored baths; luxurious linens. **Cons:** on a busy street. ⊠ *907 Truman Ave.* ☎ *305/296–5152 or 888/253–2985* ⊕ *www.azulhotels. us* ⊅ *10 rooms, 1 suite* ⚿ *In-room: Wi-Fi. In-hotel: pool, Wi-Fi hotspot, no kids under 21* ⊟ *AE, D, MC, V* ⊚ *CP.*

$$$ 🖾 **Best Western Key Ambassador Resort Inn.** You know what to expect from this chain hotel: well-maintained rooms, predictable service, and competitive prices. This one also happens to be on a 7-acre piece of property with ocean views next to the airport. Accommodations are cheerful, if uninspired, with Caribbean-style furniture and linens in coordinated tropical colors. All have screened-in balco-

nies. The palm-shaded pool looks over the Atlantic, and a covered picnic area with a large barbecue grill encourages socializing. **Pros:** big pool area; popular tiki bar. **Cons:** airport noise; lacks personality. ✉ *3755 S. Roosevelt Blvd., New Town* ☎ *305/296–3500 or 800/432–4315* ⊕ *www. keyambassador.com* ☞ *101 rooms* ♿ *In-room: refrigerator, Wi-Fi. In-hotel: restaurant, bar, pool, laundry facilities, Wi-Fi hotspot, airport shuttle, parking (no fee), no-smoking rooms* ⊟ *AE, D, DC, MC, V* ⚬ *CP.*

$$$$ 🏨 **Casa Marina Resort.** At any moment, you expect the landed
★ gentry to walk across the oceanfront lawn, just as they did
🕐 when this 13-acre resort was built back in the 1920s. Set on a private beach, where today you can have a cabana spa treatment, it has the same richly appointed lobby with beamed ceilings, polished pine floor, and original art. Guest rooms are stylishly decorated with dark wood and earth tones; bathrobes, espresso machines, iHome clock radios, and luxurious designer toiletries make it feel like boutique hotel. Two-bedroom loft suites with balconies face the ocean. The main building's ground-floor lanai rooms open onto the lawn, and the pools have a nice view of the Atlantic. **Pros:** area's nicest resort beach; historic setting; away from the crowds. **Cons:** long walk to Old Town. ✉ *1500 Reynolds St.* ☎ *305/296–3535 or 866/397–6342* ⊕ *www. casamarinaresort.com* ☞ *311 rooms, 68 suites* ♿ *In-room: safe, Wi-Fi., a/c. In-hotel: restaurant, room service, bars, tennis courts, pools, gym, beachfront, diving, water sports, bicycles, children's programs (ages 4–12), laundry service, Internet terminal, Wi-Fi hotspot* ⊟ *AE, D, DC, MC, V.*

$$$ 🏨 **Courtney's Place.** If you like kids, cats, and dogs, you'll feel right at home in this collection of accommodations ranging from cigar-maker cottages to shotgun houses. The interiors are equally varied in coloring and furnishings, but all rooms have at least a refrigerator, microwave, and coffeepot, if not a full kitchen. The family-owned property is in a residential neighborhood, though within easy walking distance of Duval Street. All rooms are not created equal here; tiny loft rooms are tucked into attic space. **Pros:** near Duval Street; fairly priced. **Cons:** small parking lot; small pool. ✉ *720 Whitemarsh La., off Petronia St.* ☎ *305/294–3480 or 800/869–4639* ⊕ *www.courtneysplacekeywest.com* ☞ *6 rooms, 2 suites, 2 efficiencies, 8 cottages* ♿ *In-room: kitchen (some), refrigerator, a/c. In-hotel: pool, bicycles, parking (free), some pets allowed* ⊟ *AE, D, MC, V* ⚬ *CP.*

$$$– ⊞**Eden House**. This 1920s rambling Key West mainstay
$$$$ hotel is high on character, low on gloss. You'll get a taste
★ of authentic Old Key West without sacrificing convenience
or comfort. Rooms come in all shapes and sizes, from
shared-bath basics to large apartments with full kitchens
and private decks or porches. The spacious outdoor area
is shaded by towering palms. Grab a book and plop in a
hammock in the outdoor library tucked into a sun-dappled
corner with a gurgling waterfall, hot tub, and potted bonsai.
Pros: sunny garden; hot tub is actually hot; daily happy
hour around the pool. **Cons:** pricey. ⊠ *1015 Fleming St.*
☎ *305/296–6868 or 800/533–5397* ⊕ *www.edenhouse.com*
⊃ *36 rooms, 8 suites* ☖ *In-room: kitchen (some), refrigera-
tor (some). In-hotel: restaurant, pool, bicycles, Internet
terminal, Wi-Fi hotspot* ▭ *MC, V.*

★ Fodor's Choice ⊠ **The Gardens Hotel**. Built in 1875, this gloriously
$$$$ shaded property covers a third of a city block in Old Town.
Here a romantic inn offers several types of accommoda-
tions, from standard rooms with garden and courtyard
views to a two-bedroom carriage-house suite. Decorated
with Bahamian plantation-style furnishings, the quiet and
elegant rooms are luxurious tropical retreats. Most have
private verandas. **Pros:** luxurious bathrooms; secluded
garden seating; free phone calls. **Cons:** hard to get reser-
vations; expensive. ⊠ *526 Angela St.* ☎ *305/294–2661 or
800/526–2664* ⊕ *www.gardenshotel.com* ⊃ *17 rooms* ☖ *In-
room: safe, refrigerator, Wi-Fi. In-hotel: bar, pool, parking
(free), no kids under 16, Wi-Fi hotspot* ▭ *AE, MC, V* ◎ *CP.*

$$–$$$ ⊞**Harborside Motel & Marina**. This little motel neatly packages
three appealing characteristics—affordability, safety, and
a pleasant location between Old Town and New Town at
Garrison Bight. Units are boxy and basic, with little patios,
ceramic-tile floors, and lots of peace and quiet. For on-the-
water living, book one of the four stationary houseboats
with shiny new interiors; each sleeps four. Sportfishing char-
ters leave from here, and there's a fish-cleaning table on the
dock. **Pros:** grills for cookouts; friendly fishing atmosphere;
boat slips. **Cons:** more than a mile from Duval Street; $10
cash key deposit. ⊠ *903 Eisenhower Dr.* ☎ *305/294–2780 or
800/501–7823* ⊕ *www.keywestharborside.com* ⊃ *7 rooms,
5 efficiencies, 4 houseboats* ☖ *In-room: kitchen (some),
refrigerator, Wi-Fi. In-hotel: pool, laundry facilities* ▭ *AE,
D, DC, MC, V.*

$$$ ⊞**Heron House Court**. This circa-1900 inn provides everyone
with a warm welcome. Its Conch-style architecture harks
back to the property's origins as a boardinghouse and cigar-

makers' cottages. Standard rooms in the main house are small, so opt for a superior room, slightly more expensive but a great deal larger. Airy, bright rooms have tiled floors and a complementary mix of antiques and reproductions, and are tastefully decorated in tropical colors. The guest rooms are nicer than the public areas, which include a pool and weathered deck. **Pros:** complimentary weekend wine hours; fluffy bathrobes. **Cons:** faces noisy Eaton Street; tiny pool. ⊠ *412 Frances St.* ☎ *305/296–4719 or 888/265–2395* ⊕ *www.heronhousecourt.com* ⮤ *3 suites, 12 rooms* ☼ *In-room: refrigerator, Wi-Fi. In-hotel: pool, no kids under 21, no-smoking rooms* ⊟ *AE, D, MC, V* ⟐*CP.*

$$$$ 🖅 **Hyatt Key West Resort and Spa.** With its own man-made beach, the Hyatt Key West is one of few resorts where you can dig your toes in the sand, then walk a short distance away to the streets of Old Town. It offers a wide range of water sports, two good restaurants, and fitness amenities—all with an eye toward keeping green. Rooms are bright and airy, with walk-in showers and rain showerheads, and balconies that overlook the Gulf. It pampers you with little extras such as down comforters and fluffy robes. **Pros:** a little bit away from the bustle of Old Town; plenty of activities. **Cons:** beach is small; cramped-feeling property; chain-hotel feel. ⊠ *601 Front St.* ☎ *305/809–1234* ⊕ *www.keywest.hyatt.com* ⮤ *118 rooms* ☼ *In-room: safe, Internet, Wi-Fi. In-hotel: 2 restaurants, room service, bars, pool, gym, spa, beachfront, diving, water sports, laundry service, parking (paid)* ⊟ *AE, D, DC, MC, V.*

$$$$ 🖅 **Island City House Hotel.** A private garden with brick walkways, tropical plants, and a canopy of palms sets this convivial guesthouse apart from the pack. The vintage-1880s Island City House has wraparound verandas, pine floors, and charm to spare. Arch House, a former carriage house, has a dramatic entry that opens into a lush courtyard. Although all suites front on busy Eaton Street, only Nos. 5 and 6 face it. A reconstructed cigar factory has become the poolside Cigar House, with spacious rooms, porches, decks, and plantation-style teak and wicker furnishings. The private tropical garden wraps around a spacious pool area. Children are welcome—a rarity in Old Town guesthouses. **Pros:** lush gardens; knowledgeable staff. **Cons:** spotty Wi-Fi service; no front-desk staff at night; some rooms are small. ⊠ *411 William St.* ☎ *305/294–5702 or 800/634–8230* ⊕ *www.islandcityhouse.com* ⮤ *24 suites* ☼ *In-room: kitchen, Wi-Fi. In-hotel: pool, bicycles, laundry facilities, Wi-Fi hotspot* ⊟ *AE, DC, MC, V* ⟐*CP.*

$$$ 🏳️ **Island House.** Geared specifically toward gay men, this hotel features a health club, a video lounge, a café and bar, and rooms in historic digs. Clothing is optional everywhere but in the gym. **Pros:** lots of privacy; just the place to get that all-over tan; free happy hour for guests. **Cons:** no women allowed. ✉ *1129 Fleming St.* ☎ *305/294–6284 or 800/890–6284* ⊕ *www.islandhousekeywest.com* ⇆ *371 rooms, 3 with shared bath* ♿ *In-room: safe, refrigerator, Wi-Fi. In-hotel: restaurant, bar, pool, Internet terminal, Wi-Fi hotspot* ▭ *AE, D, DC, MC, V.*

$$$– $$$$ 🏳️ **Key Lime Inn.** This 1854 Grand Bahama–style house on the National Register of Historic Places succeeds by offering amiable service, a great location, and simple rooms with natural-wood furnishings. The cluster of pastel-painted cottages, surrounded by white picket fences, has a residential feel, a bit like a beach colony without the beach, or the backlot of a movie set. The Garden Cottages have one room; a few include a porch or balcony. Some rooms in the historic Maloney House have a porch or patio. **Pros:** free parking; some rooms have private outdoor spaces. **Cons:** standard rooms are pricey; pool faces a busy street; mulch-covered paths. ✉ *725 Truman Ave.* ☎ *305/294–5229 or 800/549–4430* ⊕ *www.keylimeinn.com* ⇆ *37 rooms* ♿ *In-room: safe, refrigerator (some), Internet, Wi-Fi. In-hotel: pool, Wi-Fi hotspot, parking (free)* ▭ *AE, D, MC, V* ⫟*CP.*

$$– $$$ 🏳️ **Key West Bed and Breakfast/The Popular House.** Local art— ★ large, splashy canvases and a Gauguinesque mural—decorates the walls, while handmade textiles (owner Jody Carlson is a talented weaver) drape chairs, couches, and beds at this historic home. There are accommodations for every budget, but the owners reason that budget travelers deserve as pleasant an experience (and lavish a tropical Continental breakfast) as their well-heeled counterparts. Less expensive rooms burst with bright colors (hand-painted dressers add a whimsical flourish), and balconies on the second-floor rooms overlook the gardens. Spacious, and more expensive, third-floor rooms are decorated with a paler palette and original furniture. **Pros:** lots of art; tiled outdoor shower; hot tub and sauna area is a welcome hangout. **Cons:** some rooms are small; pool is a small "dipping" pool. ✉ *415 William St.* ☎ *305/296–7274 or 800/438–6155* ⊕ *www.keywestbandb.com* ⇆ *8 rooms, 6 with bath* ♿ *In-room: no phone, no TV, Wi-Fi (some). In-hotel: pool, bicycles, Wi-Fi hotspot, no kids under 18* ▭ *AE, D, DC, MC, V* ⫟*CP.*

5

$$$$ ☒ **Key West Marriott Beachside**. This new hotel, branded a
Marriott in 2008, vies for convention business with the
biggest ballroom in Key West. It also appeals to families with its spacious condo units decorated with impec-
cable good taste. Designer furnishings reflect the resort's
waterfront location. Frette linens on the beds, real china in
the kitchens, and marble hot tubs add touches of luxury.
Rooms have spiral staircases down to the gardens and up
to the rooftop sundecks. Families enjoy the beach and pool
area. Complimentary shuttles take guests to Old Town and
the airport. **Pros:** private beach; poolside cabanas. **Cons:**
small beach; can't walk to Old Town; cookie-cutter facade.
☒ *3841 N. Roosevelt Blvd., New Town* ☎ *305/296–8100 or
800/546–0885* ⊕ *www.beachsidekeywest.com* ⌨ *93 1-bed-
room suites, 9 2-bedroom suites, 27 3-bedroom suites* ⌂ *In-
room: kitchen (some), Internet. In-hotel: 2 restaurants,
room service, bars, pool, gym, Wi-Fi hotspot, parking
(paid)* ⊟ *AE, D, DC, MC, V.*

$$$ ☒ **La Pensione**. Hospitality and period furnishings make this
1891 home, once owned by a cigar executive, a wonderful
glimpse into Key West life in the late 19th century. Each
of the rooms has a private bath and king-size or double
beds. All but one have a sitting area—the exception being
a handicapped-accessible room. None have televisions, but
not to worry, there's plenty of entertainment on nearby
Duval Street. Rates include daily Continental breakfast
in the dining room or on the veranda. **Pros:** pine-paneled
walls; off-street parking; some rooms have wraparound
porches. **Cons:** street-facing rooms are noisy; baths need
updating. ☒ *809 Truman Ave.* ☎ *305/292–9923 or 800/893–
1193* ⊕ *www.lapensione.com* ⌨ *9 rooms* ⌂ *In-room: no
TV, Wi-Fi. In-hotel: pool, parking (free), no kids under 18*
⊟ *AE, D, MC, V* ◉ *CP.*

★ Fodor'sChoice ☒ **Marquesa Hotel**. In a town that prides itself
$$$$ on its laid-back luxury, this complex of four restored 1884
houses stands out. Guests—typically shoeless in Marquesa
robes—relax near two richly landscaped pools, rock water-
falls, and peaceful gardens. Elegant rooms surround a
courtyard, and have antique and reproduction furnishings,
earthy tones with black-and-white accents, marble baths,
and outdoor sitting areas. Six off-site cottages are also for
rent. The lobby resembles a Victorian parlor, with Audu-
bon prints, vases overflowing with flowers, and photos
of early Key West. **Pros:** elegant setting; romantic atmo-
sphere; turndown service. **Cons:** street-facing rooms can
be noisy; expensive rates. ☒ *600 Fleming St.* ☎ *305/292–*

*1919 or 800/869–4631 ⊕ www.marquesa.com ⋙ 27 rooms
⌂ In-room: a/c, safe, refrigerator, DVD, Wi-Fi. In-hotel:
restaurant, room service, pools, laundry service, Internet
terminal, Wi-Fi hotspot, parking (free), no kids under 14
⊟ AE, DC, MC, V.*

$$$ ⌧ **Merlin Guesthouse.** Key West guesthouses don't usually
★ welcome families, but this laid-back jumble of rooms
and suites is an exception. Accommodations in the 1930s
Simonton House, with four-poster beds, are most suitable
for couples. The one- and two-bedroom suites are popu-
lar with families. Bright, roomy cottages are perfect if you
want a bit more privacy. Get a room in the back if you are
bothered by noise. The leafy courtyard and pool area are
where guests hang out day and night. **Pros:** good location
near Duval Street; good rates. **Cons:** neighbor noise; com-
mon areas are dated; street parking. ⊠ *811 Simonton St.*
☎ *305/296–3336 or 800/642–4753* ⊕ *www.merlinguest-
house.com* ⋙ *10 rooms, 6 suites, 4 cottages* ⌂ *In-room:
no phone, safe, kitchen (some), refrigerator (some). In-hotel:
pool, Wi-Fi hotspot* ⊟ *AE, D, MC, V* ⅋ *CP.*

$$$– ⌧ **Mermaid & the Alligator.** An enchanting combination of
$$$$ flora and fauna makes this 1904 Victorian house a wel-
★ coming retreat. The property is filled with palms, ban-
yans, birds of paradise, poincianas, cages of colorful, live
parrots, and swarms of butterflies. Rooms are Caribbean
colonial–inspired, with wood-slat floors, elegant trim, and
French doors. The color scheme—key lime, cantaloupe,
and other rich colors—couldn't be more evocative of the
Keys. Some downstairs rooms open onto the deck, pool,
and gardens designed by one of the resident owners, a
landscape designer. Upstairs rooms overlook the gardens.
A full breakfast is served poolside, and guests can take
advantage of complimentary bottled waters, soda, and
evening wine. **Pros:** hot plunge pool; massage pavilion;
island-getaway feel. **Cons:** minimum stay required (length
depends on season); dark public areas; plastic lawn chairs.
⊠ *729 Truman Ave.* ☎ *305/294–1894 or 800/773–1894*
⊕ *www.kwmermaid.com* ⋙ *9 rooms* ⌂ *In-room: no phone,
no TV, Wi-Fi. In-hotel: pool, Internet terminal, no kids
under 16* ⊟ *AE, MC, V* ⅋ *BP.*

$$$$ ⌧ **Ocean Breeze Inn.** What this simple South Beach area motel
lacks in style it makes up for in value. Rooms, with peachy
floral colors and wicker furniture, are clustered around a
tiny pool in one-story cement-block strips. Some are quite
spacious, with high ceilings, kitchenettes, and dining-sitting
areas. **Pros:** early (2 PM) check-in; clean and spacious rooms;

staff remembers your name. **Cons:** bland decor; small pool; no staff after 6 PM. ⊠ *625 South St.* ☎ *305/296–2829 or 877/879–2362* ⊕ *www.oceanbreezeinn.com* ⇝ *15 rooms* ⬧ *In-room: kitchen (some), Wi-Fi. In-hotel: pool, Wi-Fi hotspot* ⊟ *D, MC, V* ⧖ *CP.*

$$$$ ⛱ **Ocean Key Resort & Spa.** A pool and lively open-air bar
★ and restaurant sit on Sunset Pier, a popular place to watch the sun sink into the horizon. Toast the day's end from private balconies that extend from spacious rooms that are both stylish and homey. Thirteen different room types range from junior suites to bedroom suites, all with individualized design elements such as hand-painted furnishings, four-poster or sleigh beds, wooden chests, and lavish whirlpool tubs. Its second-floor elegant restaurant is cleverly named Hot Tin Roof, a reference to its construction as well as to Tennessee Williams' Key West connection. **Pros:** well-trained staff; lively pool scene; best spa on the island. **Cons:** confusing layout; too bustling for some, especially at sunset. ⊠ *Zero Duval St.* ☎ *305/296–7701 or 800/328–9815* ⊕ *www.oceankey.com* ⇝ *100 suites* ⬧ *In-room: kitchen (some), refrigerator, Wi-Fi. In-hotel: 2 restaurants, room service, bars, pool, spa, diving, water sports, bicycles, laundry service, parking (paid), Wi-Fi hotspot* ⊟ *AE, D, DC, MC, V.*

$$$$ ⛱ **Parrot Key Resort.** The same people who created Tran-
★ quility Bay in Marathon opened this high-end Key West resort in 2008. It feels like an old-fashioned beach community, with picket fences and rocking-chair porches. Three-story town houses feature a modern kitchen on the first floor and two or three bedrooms on the second and third floors. Mangroves fringe the man-made beach that edges Florida Bay. **Pros:** four pools; finely appointed units; access to marina and other facilities at three sister properties in Marathon. **Cons:** outside of walking distance to Old Town and no transportation provided; expensive; hefty ($24 per night) resort fee. ⊠ *2801 N. Roosevelt Blvd., New Town* ☎ *305/809–2200* ⊕ *www.parrotkeyresort.com* ⇝ *44 2-bedroom town houses, 30 3-bedroom town houses* ⬧ *In-room: kitchen, DVD, Wi-Fi. In-hotel: restaurant, bar, pools, beachfront, no-smoking rooms* ⊟ *AE, D, MC, V.*

$$$ ⛱ **Pearl's Rainbow.** This guesthouse, which caters to lesbians and gay-friendly women, occupies an 1886 cigar factory. It's home to Pearl's Patio, a women-only bar, which also serves breakfast, lunch, and evening snacks. Rooms range from basic to deluxe, and are comfortable, clean, and well appointed. Those without their own refrigerator have access to shared kitchens. **Pros:** full breakfast; plenty of privacy. **Cons:** no men allowed; bar attracts late-night partiers. ✉ *525 United St.* ☎ *305/292–1450 or 800/749–6696* ⊕ *www.pearlsrainbow.com* ⇨ *32 rooms, 2 efficiencies, 4 suites* ⌂ *In-room: kitchen (some), refrigerator (some), Wi-Fi. In-hotel: a/c, restaurant, bar, pools, Internet terminal, Wi-Fi hotspot* ⊟ *AE, D, MC, V* ⊙ *BP.*

$$$$ ⊡ **Pier House Resort and Caribbean Spa.** The location—on a
★ quiet stretch of beach at the foot of Duval—is ideal as a buffer from and gateway to the action. Its sprawling complex of weathered gray buildings includes an original Conch house. The courtyard is riotous with tall coconut palms and hibiscus blossoms, and rooms are cozy and colorful, with a water, pool, or garden view. Six top-of-the-line suites extend over the water with sunset views. Rooms nearest the public areas can be noisy. **Pros:** beautiful beach; good location; nice spa. **Cons:** lots of conventions; poolside rooms are small. ✉ *1 Duval St.* ☎ *305/296–4600 or 800/327–8340* ⊕ *www.pierhouse.com* ⇨ *113 rooms, 29 suites* ⌂ *In-room: refrigerator, Internet, Wi-Fi (some). In-hotel: 2 restaurants, room service, bars, pool, gym, spa, beachfront, bicycles, laundry service, Wi-Fi hotspot* ⊟ *AE, D, DC, MC, V.*

$$$$ ⊡ **The Reach Resort.** Embracing Key West's only natural
★ beach, this recently reinvented and reopened full-service resort has its roots in the 1980s, when locals rallied against the loss of the topless beach it displaced. As a tip of the hat to the city's bohemian spirit, the resort devotes a portion to topless sunbathing. And then there's the Strip House, its naughty little steak house with nude images and a bordello feel. Top luxury prevails these days from turndown service and plushly lined seersucker robes in the room to life-sized chess and bocci in the courtyard and a pool concierge delivering popsicles and drinks du jour. In addition to its own facilities, guests are privy to the spa treatments, tennis, and other amenities at sister resort Casa Marina nearby. The private pier-gazebo makes a perfect spot for weddings and watching the sunrise. **Pros:** removed from Duval hubbub; great sunrise views; pullout sofas in most rooms. **Cons:** $20 per day per room resort fee; expensive. ✉ *1435 Simonton St.* ☎ *305/296–5000 or 888/318–4316* ⊕ *www.reachresort.com* ⇨ *150 rooms, 76 suites* ⌂ *In-room: safe, refrigerator, Wi-Fi. In-hotel: restaurant, room service, bars, pools, gym, beachfront, water sports, laundry service, Internet terminal, Wi-Fi hotspot, parking (paid), some pets allowed (fee)* ⊟ *AE, D, DC, MC, V.*

5

$$$$ ⚇ **Simonton Court.** A small world all of its own, this lodging
★   makes you feel deliciously sequestered from Key West's
crasser side, but close enough to get there on foot. The
"basic" rooms are in an old cigar factory, each with its
own unique decor. There's also a restored shotgun house
and cottages. But top-of-the-line units occupy a Victorian
home and the town house facing the property's pool and
brick-paved breakfast courtyard. **Pros:** lots of privacy;
well-appointed accommodations; friendly staff. **Cons:**
minimum stays required in high season. ✉ *320 Simonton
St.* ☎ *305/294–6386 or 800/944–2687* ⊕ *www.simonton-
court.com* ⇆ *17 rooms, 6 suites, 6 cottages* ♿ *In-room:
safe, kitchen (some), refrigerator, Wi-Fi. In-hotel: pools,
no kids under 18, Wi-Fi hotspot* ⊟ *D, DC, MC, V* ⦿ *CP.*

$$$– ⚇ **Southernmost Hotel.** This hotel's location on the quiet end
$$$$ of Duval means you don't have to deal with the hustle
and bustle of downtown unless you want to—it's within a
20-minute walk (but around sunset, this end of town gets
its share of car and foot traffic). Cookie-cutter rooms are
spacious, bright, and airy, and have cottage-style furnish-
ings and the required tropical color schemes. Grab a cold
drink from the Tiki Hut bar and join the crowd around the
pool, or venture across the street to the beach, where there's
a restaurant and a sister beach resort. **Pros:** pool attracts
a lively crowd; access to nearby properties; free parking.
Cons: public beach is small; can get crowded around the
pool and in public areas. ✉ *1319 Duval St.* ☎ *305/296–6577
or 800/354–4455* ⊕ *www.southernmostresorts.com* ⇆ *127
rooms* ♿ *In-room: safe, refrigerator, Wi-Fi. In-hotel: pool,
laundry facilities, Wi-Fi hotspot* ⊟ *AE, D, DC, MC, V.*

$$–$$$ ⚇ **Speakeasy Inn.** During Prohibition, Raul Vasquez made
this place popular by smuggling in liquor from Cuba. Today
the booze is legal, and there's a daily happy hour so you can
fully appreciate it. The Speakeasy Inn is still well known,
only now its reputation is for having reasonably priced
rooms within walking distance of the beach. Accommo-
dations have bright-white walls offset by bursts of color
in rugs, pillows, and seat cushions. Queen-size beds and
tables are fashioned from salvaged pine. The rooms are
basic, but some have nice touches like claw-foot tubs.
Room 1A has a deck that's good for people-watching.
Pros: good location; reasonable rates; high-quality rum
bar attached. **Cons:** no pool; basic decor. ✉ *1117 Duval
St.* ☎ *305/296–2680* ⊕ *www.speakeasyinn.com* ⇆ *2 suites,
4 studios* ♿ *In-room: refrigerator, Wi-Fi. In-hotel: Internet
terminal, Wi-Fi hotspot* ⊟ *AE, D, MC, V* ⦿ *CP.*

THE HOLIDAYS KEY WEST STYLE

On New Year's Eve, Key West celebrates the turning of the calendar page with three separate ceremonies that parody New York's dropping-of-the-ball drama. Here they let fall a 6-foot conch shell from Sloppy Joe's Bar, a pirate wench from the towering mast of a tall ship at the Historic Seaport, and a drag queen (elegantly decked out in a ball gown and riding an oversize red high-heel shoe) at Bourbon Street Pub. You wouldn't expect any less from America's most outrageous city.

Key West is one of the nation's biggest party towns, so the celebrations here take on a colorful hue. In keeping with Key West's rich maritime heritage, its month-long Bight Before Christmas begins Thanksgiving Eve at Key West Bight. The Lighted Boat Parade creates a quintessential Florida spectacle with live music and decorated vessels of all shapes and sizes.

Some years, Tennessee Williams Theatre hosts a Key West version of the Nutcracker. In this unorthodox retelling, the heroine sails to a coral reef and is submerged in a diving bell. (What? No sugarplum fairies?) Between Christmas and New Year's Day, the Holiday House and Garden Tour is another yuletide tradition.

★ Fodor's Choice ⚑ **Sunset Key Guest Cottages, a Westin Resort.** This **$$$$** private island retreat feels completely cut off from the world, yet you're just minutes away from the action. Board a 10-minute launch to 27-acre Sunset Key, where you'll find sandy beaches, swaying palms, flowering gardens, and a delicious sense of privacy. The comforts are first-class at the cluster of one- to four-bedroom cottages at the water's edge. Baked goods, freshly squeezed juice, and a newspaper are delivered each morning. Each of the accommodations has a kitchen, and the resort offers a grocery shopping service (for a fee, of course). You can use all the facilities at the Westin Key West Resort & Marina in Old Town, but be warned: you may never want to leave Sunset Key and its great restaurant, pretty pool, and very civilized beach complete with attendants and cabanas. In 2010 it opened a new three-treatment-room, full-service spa. **Pros:** peace and quiet; roomy verandas; free 24-hour shuttle. **Cons:** luxury doesn't come cheap. ⊠*245 Front St.* ☎*305/292–5300 or 888/477–7786* ⊕*www.westinsunsetkeycottages.com* ⇱*39 cottages* ⌂*In-room: safe, kitchen, DVD, Internet, Wi-Fi.*

LODGING ALTERNATIVES

The Key West Innkeepers Association is an umbrella organization for dozens of local properties. Vacation Rentals Key West lists historic cottages, homes, and condominiums for rent. Rent Key West Vacations specializes in renting vacation homes and condos for a week or longer. Vacation Key West lists all kinds of properties throughout Key West. **Key West Innkeepers Association** (✉ 316A Simonton St., Key West ☎ 305/295-1334 or 800/492-1911 ⊕ www. keywestinns.com). **Vacation Rentals Key West** (✉ 1511 Truman Ave., Key West ☎ 305/292-7997 or 800/621-9405 ⊕ www. keywestvacations.com). **Rent Key West Vacations** (✉ 1075 Duval St., Ste. C11, Key West ☎ 305/294-0990 or 800/833-7368 ⊕ www. rentkeywest.com). **Vacation Key West** (✉ 100 Grinnell St., Key West ☎ 305/295-9500 or 800/595-5397 ⊕ www.vaca- tionkw.com).

In-hotel: restaurant, room service, bars, tennis courts, pool, gym, spa, beachfront, laundry service, Internet terminal, Wi-Fi hotspot, parking (paid ⊟AE, D, DC, MC, V ⃝CP.

$$$$ ⌧ **Westin Key West Resort & Marina.** This waterfront resort's two three-story, Keys-style buildings huddle around its 37-slip marina in the middle of Old Town. It has all the elegant touches associated with the Westin name, including the Heavenly Bed and Starbucks coffee in the rooms. As a sister resort to Sunset Key, Westin offers guests limited access to the private island resort via a short shuttle boat ride. Most of the rooms, which are large by Key West standards, look out on the Gulf of Mexico. All have earthy color schemes, and some have jetted tubs. **Pros:** good location; bar and restaurant overlook Mallory Square; access to Sunset Key; free Wi-Fi. **Cons:** feels too big for Key West; often crowded; conference clientele. ✉ 245 Front St. ☎ 305/294–4000 ⊕ www.westin.com/keywest ⤴ 146 rooms, 32 suites ⅙ In-room: safe, Wi-Fi. In-hotel: a/c, 4 restaurants, room service, bars, pool, gym, water sports, concierge, Internet terminal, Wi-Fi hotspots, parking (fee), some pets allowed ⊟AE, D, DC, MC, V.

$$$ ⌧ **Westwinds Inn.** This cluster of historic gingerbread-trimmed houses has individually decorated rooms that make you feel right at home. The buildings spread throughout luxuriant gardens with two swimming pools (one heated) just a couple of blocks from the Historic Key West Seaport.

The library provides a spot to read or grab snacks from the communal refrigerator and microwave. The poolside breakfast is generous. **Pros:** away from Old Town's bustle; lots of character; affordable rates. **Cons:** small lobby; confusing layout; a long walk from Duval Street. ⊠*914 Eaton St.* ☏*305/296–4440 or 800/788–4150* ⊕ *www.westwindskey-west.com* ⟿*21 rooms, 4 suites* ⚬ *In-room: Wi-Fi. In-hotel: pools, laundry facilities, Wi-Fi hotspot, no kids under age 1* ⊟*D, MC, V* ⊚*CP.*

NIGHTLIFE AND THE ARTS

NIGHTLIFE

Rest up: Much of what happens in Key West does so after dark. Open your mind and have a stroll. Scruffy street performers strum next to dogs in sunglasses. Characters wearing parrots or iguanas try to sell you your photo with their pet. Brawls tumble out the doors of Sloppy Joe's. Drag queens strut across stages in Joan Rivers garb. Tattooed men lick whipped cream off women's body parts. And margaritas flow like a Jimmy Buffett tune.

BEST OF THE BARS. Southernmost Scavenger Hunt's "Best of the Bars" challenge has teams of two to five touring the bars of Key West for clues, libations, and prizes. It hosts the event at 7 PM most Fridays, Saturdays, and Sundays, starting at Sloppy Joe's. The cost is $20 per person. For information, call ☏ *305/292–9994* or visit ⊕ *www.keywesthunt.com.*

BARS AND LOUNGES
Capt. Tony's Saloon (⊠*428 Greene St.* ☏*305/294–1838* ⊕*www.capttonyssaloon.com*) was the original Sloppy Joe's in the mid-1930s, when Hemingway was a regular. Later, a young Jimmy Buffett sang here and made this watering hole famous in his song "Last Mango in Paris." Bands play nightly.

Ride the mechanical bucking bull, listen to live bands croon cry-in-your-beer tunes, and grab some pretty decent chow at the indoor-outdoor spread known as **Cowboy Bill's Honky Tonk Saloon** (⊠*610½ Duval St.* ☏*305/295–8219* ⊕*www.cowboybillskw.com*). Wednesday brings—we kid you not— Sexy Bikini Bull Riding.

No matter your mood, **Durty Harry's** (⊠ *208 Duval St.* ☎ *305/296–5513* ⊕ *www.ricksanddurtyharrys.com*) can fill the bill. The megasize entertainment complex has live music in a variety of indoor-outdoor bars, including Rick's Dance Club Wine & Martini Bar and the Red Garter strip club.

Perhaps one of Duval's more unusual and intriguing watering holes, **The Garden of Eden** (⊠ *224 Duval St.* ☎ *305/396–4565* ⊕ *www.bullkeywest.com*) sits atop the Bull & Whistle saloon and has a clothing-optional policy. Most drinkers are looky-lous, but some actually bare it all.

Pause for a libation at the open-air **Green Parrot Bar** (⊠ *601 Whitehead St., at Southard St.* ☎ *305/294–6133* ⊕ *www. greenparrot.com*). Built in 1890, the bar is said to be Key West's oldest, and with its location at mile marker 0 advertises itself as "the first and last bar on U.S. 1. The sometimes-rowdy saloon has locals outnumbering out-of-towners, especially when bands play.

Belly up to the bar for a cold mug of the signature Hog's Breath Lager at the infamous **Hog's Breath Saloon** (⊠ *400 Front St.* ☎ *305/296–4222* ⊕ *www.hogsbreath.com*), a must-stop on the Key West bar crawl. Live bands play daily 1 PM–2 AM.

A youngish, touristy crowd, sprinkled with aging Parrot Heads, frequents **Margaritaville Café** (⊠ *500 Duval St.* ☎ *305/292–1435* ⊕ *www.margaritaville.com*), owned by Key West resident and recording star Jimmy Buffett, who has been known to make surprise appearances here. The drink of choice is, of course, a margarita, made with Jimmy's own brand of Margaritaville tequila. There's live music nightly, as well as lunch and dinner.

Nightlife at the **Pier House** (⊠ *1 Duval St.* ☎ *305/296–4600* or *800/327–8340* ⊕ *www.pierhouse.com*) begins with a steel-drum band to celebrate the sunset on the beach (on select Fridays and Saturdays), then moves indoors to the Wine Galley piano bar for live jazz.

The **Schooner Wharf Bar** (⊠ *202 William St.* ☎ *305/292–3302* ⊕ *www.schoonerwharf.com*), an open-air waterfront bar and grill in the historic seaport district, retains its funky Key West charm and hosts live entertainment daily. Happy hour begins at 7 AM—and no, that isn't a misprint. Beer and eggs anyone? Its margarita ranks among Key West's best.

There's history and good times at **Sloppy Joe's** (✉ *201 Duval St.* ☎ *305/294–5717* ⊕ *www.sloppyjoes.com*), the successor to a famous 1937 speakeasy named for its founder, Captain Joe Russell. Decorated with Hemingway memorabilia and marine flags, the bar is popular with travelers, and is full and noisy all the time. A Sloppy Joe's T-shirt is a de rigueur Key West souvenir, and the gift shop sells them like crazy.

The Top (✉ *430 Duval St.* ☎ *305/296–2991* ⊕ *www.laconchakeywest.com*) is on the seventh floor of the La Concha Crowne Plaza and is one of the best places in town to view the sunset and enjoy live entertainment.

Love karaoke? Get it out of your system at **Two Friends Patio Lounge** (✉ *512 Front St.* ☎ *305/296–3124* ⊕ *www.twofriendskeywest.com*), the self-proclaimed "Key West King of Karoake." The singing starts nightly at 8:30 PM.

Virgilio's (✉ *524 Duval St.* ☎ *305/296–8118* ⊕ *www.virgilioskeywest.com*) serves chilled martinis—from classic to flavors such as Milky Way and chocolate-chip cookie—to the soothing tempo of live jazz and blues nightly.

GAY AND LESBIAN BARS

Key West's largest gay bar, **Aqua** (✉ *711 Duval St.* ☎ *305/294–0555* ⊕ *www.aquakeywest.com*) hosts drag shows, karaoke contests, and live entertainment at three bars, including one outside on the patio.

Pick your entertainment at the **Bourbon Street Complex** (✉ *724 Duval St.* ☎ *305/293–9800* ⊕ *www.bourbonstpub.com*), a club within an all-male guesthouse. There are 10 video screens along with dancers grooving to the latest music spun by DJs at the Bourbon Street Pub.

Part of a men's resort, **Island House Café + Bar** (✉ *Island House, 1129 Fleming St.* ☎ *305/294–6284 or 800/890–6284* ⊕ *www.islandhousekeywest.com*) serves frozen and other cocktails along with creative cuisine in tropical gardens with a pool where clothing is optional. It is open 24 hours.

LaTeDa Hotel and Bar (✉ *1125 Duval St.* ☎ *305/296–6706* ⊕ *www.lateda.com*) hosts female impersonators (catch Christopher Peterson when he's on stage) and riotously funny cabaret shows nightly in the Crystal Room Cabaret Lounge. Gays and non-gays both enjoy the shows. There are also live entertainment nightly, including the popular local singer Lenore Troia, in the Terrace Garden Bar and smooth piano jazz and pricey martinis in the ultracool lounge bar.

Margarita Madness

Mojitos, martinis, and caipirinhas may be the popular drinks in Miami's South Beach, but in Key West the margarita Jimmy Buffett crooned about is still alive and well.

Every bar and club serves them, either the classic version or in dozens of variations. Every bartender claims to make the best. Here are some that rank tops in their category. At the **Half Shell Raw Bar**, the Raw Bar Rita, made with 1800 Sauza Silver Tequila and a splash of Patrón Citronge, has a funky green glow but good tartness. The Pama Rita, which the menu claims is "for the health nut," is much prettier, dyed and flavored with a splash of red Pama liqueur, and also fueled with Sauza Silver. It scores best in the novelty category.

Although **El Meson de Pepe** brags about its mojitos, its Gold Margarita, made with El Jimador Reposado, is no slouch. It goes especially well with a basket of Cuban bread served with addictive red and green dipping sauces, so it rates tops for its ability to play well with food.

At Bagatelle's **Toucan Bar** the Patrón's Margarita, named for its brand of top-shelf tequila, gets points for being smooth, almost creamy. It's the perfect balance of tart and sweet. The view of Duval Street adds to the enjoyment.

At **Mangoes**, the Mangorita is naturally the signature drink. Very tropical, but made with Cuervo and Marie Brizard, it ranks in the "tourist drink" category.

The Conch-a-Rita at **Conch Republic Seafood Company** pours on the Herradura tequila with a splash of Cointreau. This is a strong contender in the classic category.

At Jimmy Buffett's **Margaritaville** one would expect high competition. Buffett on the stereo makes a margarita go down just right, with or without a shaker of salt. Jimmy's own brand of gold Margaritaville tequila goes into the potent Uptown Margarita, topped with a float of Gran Gala.

Schooner Wharf's Schoonerita takes top rating in the classic class. The bartender shakes the cocktail and squeezes in a healthy dose of real lime juice at the end. Made with Sauza tequila, it comes served in a proper glass birdbath–shaped vessel, although this one has a stem in the shape of a cactus. (South-of-the-border kitsch and margaritas go well together.)

—Chelle Koster Walton

Pearl's Patio (⊠*Pearl's Rainbow, 525 United St., between Duval and Simonton Sts.* ☎*305/293–9805 Ext. 156 or 800/749–6696* ⊕*www.pearlsrainbow.com*) is Key West's only all-female bar. It features a full range of drinks, a menu of light dishes, and nightly women's activities.

THE ARTS

Catch the classics and the latest art, independent, and foreign films shown daily by the **Key West Film Society** (⊠*416 Eaton St.* ☎*305/295–9493* ⊕*www.tropiccinema.com*) in the two-screen Tropic Cinema theater.

Sebrina Alfonso directs the **Key West Symphony** (⊠*Tennessee Williams Fine Arts Center, 5901 College Rd.* ☎*305/292–1774* ⊕*www.keywestsymphony.com*) during the winter season.

With more than 30 years' experience, the **Red Barn Theatre** (⊠*319 Duval St.* ☎*305/296–9911 or 866/870–9911* ⊕*www.redbarntheatre.com*), a small professional theater, performs dramas, comedies, and musicals, including works by new playwrights.

On Stock Island, the **Tennessee Williams Fine Arts Center** (⊠*Florida Keys Community College, 5901 College Rd.* ☎*305/296–1520* ⊕*www.tennesseewilliamstheatre.com*) presents chamber music, dance, jazz concerts, and dramatic and musical plays with major stars, as well as other performing arts events.

Home to the Key West Players, the community-run **Waterfront Playhouse** (⊠*Mallory Sq.* ☎*305/294–5015* ⊕*www. waterfrontplayhouse.org*) is a mid-1850s wrecker's warehouse that was converted into a 180-seat regional theater presenting comedy and drama from December to June. It claims to be Florida's longest continuously running theater company.

SCULPTURE KEY WEST. **Key West bursts with art, especially every year between January and April, when artists unveil their latest works at two exhibitions in Fort Zachary Taylor State Park and West Martello Tower. More than 30 artists from around the country are selected to bring their contemporary sculpture for outdoor exhibitions. In years past, sculptures have ranged from a dinosaur surfacing in a pond and a giant Key West chicken to heads floating in the water and abstract formations suggesting sea and seaside vegetation.**

SPORTS AND THE OUTDOORS

Unlike the rest of the region, Key West isn't known primarily for outdoor pursuits. But everyone should devote at least half a day to relaxing on a boat tour, heading out on a fishing expedition, or pursuing some other adventure at sea. The ultimate excursion is a boat or seaplane trip to Dry Tortugas National Park for snorkeling and exploring Fort Jefferson. Other excursions cater to nature lovers, scuba divers, and snorkelers, and folks who would just like to get out in the water and enjoy the scenery and sunset. For those who prefer their recreation land-based, biking is the way to go. Hiking is limited, but walking the streets of Old Town provides plenty of exercise.

BIKING

Key West was practically made for bicycles, but don't let that lull you into a false sense of security. Narrow and one-way streets along with car traffic result in several bike accidents a year. Some hotels rent or lend bikes to guests; others will refer you to a nearby shop and reserve a bike for you. Rentals usually start at about $12 a day, but some places also rent by the half-day. ■ TIP→ Lock up; bikes—and porch chairs!—are favorite targets for local thieves.

Eaton Bikes (⊠ 830 Eaton St. ☎ 305/295–0057 ⊕ www.eatonbikes.com) has tandem, three-wheel, and children's bikes in addition to the standard beach cruisers ($18 for first day) and seven-speed cruisers ($18). It delivers free to all Key West rentals.

A&M Rentals (⊠ 523 Truman Ave. ☎ 305/294–0399 ⊕ www.amscooterskeywest.com) rents beach cruisers with large baskets for $10 a day. Rates for scooters start at $30. Look for the huge American flag on the roof.

Moped Hospital (⊠ 601 Truman Ave. ☎ 305/296–3344 or 866/296–1625 ⊕ www.mopedhospital.com) supplies balloon-tire bikes with yellow safety baskets for adults and kids ($12 per day), as well as mopeds ($35) and double-seater scooters ($55).

Paradise Scooter Rentals (⊠ 112 Fitzpatrick St. ☎ 305/923–6063 ⊕ www.paradisescooterrentals.com) rents bikes starting at $8 for two hours and scooters for $50–$65 a day.

BOATING

Key West is surrounded by marinas, so it's easy to find what you're looking for, whether it's sailing with dolphins or paddling in the mangroves.

At **Key West Eco-Tours** (✉ *Historic Seaport* ☎ 305/294–7245 ⊕ *www.javacatcharters.com*) the sail-kayak-snorkel excursions take you into backcountry flats and mangrove forests. The 4½-hour trip costs $95 per person and includes lunch. Sunset sails ($295) and private charters ($495) are also available.

The *Schooner Liberty* (✉ *Schooner Wharf at the Historic Seaport* ☎ 305/292–0332 ⊕ *www.libertyfleet.com*) makes a dramatic statement as it passes Mallory Square. In addition to the very popular sunset cruises ($57), the 80-foot tall ship also does two-hour morning and afternoon sails ($35). Even more eye-catching, the 125-foot multi-masted *Liberty Clipper* hosts dinner and music excursions on Tuesday, Thursday, and Sunday. The cost is $79 for 2½ hours; two-hour sunset voyages with drinks and appetizers only are offered Wednesday, Friday, and Saturday for $65.

Sunset Culinaire Tours (✉ *5555 College Rd.* ☎ 305/296–0982 ⊕ *www.sunsetculinaire.com*) serves a full menu of gourmet meals with fine wine and beer aboard a sleek cruising yacht every evening at sunset. The cost is $85 per person.

FISHING

Any number of local fishing guides can take you to where the big ones are biting, either in the backcountry for snapper and snook or to the deep water for the marlins and shark that brought Hemingway here in the first place.

★ **Florida Fish Finder** (✉ *5555 College Rd., Stock Island* ☎ 800/878–3474 ⊕ *www.floridafishfinder.com*) schedules two- and three-day fishing adventures into the Dry Tortugas in up to 300 feet of water. Their maximum load is 36 anglers at a cost of $425–$525 each, including overnight berths. Meals and rod rental are extra.

Key West Bait & Tackle (✉ *241 Margaret St.* ☎ 305/292–1961 ⊕ *www.keywestbaitandtackle.com*) carries live bait, frozen bait, and fishing equipment. It also has the Live Bait Lounge, where you can sip ice-cold beer while telling fish tales.

Key West Pro Guides (✉ *G-31 Miriam St.* ☎ *866/259–4205*
⊕ *www.keywestproguides.com*) has several different trips,
including flats and backcountry fishing ($425 for a half day)
and reef and offshore fishing ($550 for half day).

GOLFING

Not in the least a golfing destination, Key West does have
one course on Stock Island. Make your tee times early in
season.

Key West Resort Golf Course (✉ *6450 E. College Rd.* ☎ *305/
294–5232* ⊕ *www.keywestgolf.com*) is an 18-hole, par
70 course on the bay side of Stock Island; greens fees are
$70–$95.

KAYAKING

At **Key West Eco-Tours** (✉ *Historic Seaport, 100 Grinnell St.*
☎ *305/294–7245* ⊕ *keywestecotours.co*), the sail-kayak-
snorkel excursions take you into backcountry flats and
mangrove forests. The 4½-hour trip costs $95 per person
and includes lunch. Sunset sails and private charters are
also available.

Lazy Dog Kayak Guides (✉ *5114 Overseas Hwy., Key West*
☎ *305/295–9898* ⊕ *www.lazydog.com*) runs four-hour
guided sea-kayak-snorkel tours around the mangrove
islands just east of Key West. The $60 charge covers trans-
portation, bottled water, a snack, and supplies, including
snorkeling gear. A $35 two-hour guided kayak tour is
also available.

The latest Florida hybrid water sport involves a surfboard
and a paddle, a Hawaii transplant known as stand-up
paddleboarding. **Sup Key West** (✉ *110 Grinell St.* ☎ *305/240–
1426* ⊕ *www.supkeywest.com*) does lessons and tours of the
estuaries for $40–$45. Call ahead to make arrangements.

SCUBA DIVING AND SNORKELING

The Florida Keys National Marine Sanctuary extends
along Key West and beyond to the Dry Tortugas. Key
West National Wildlife Refuge further protects the pristine
waters. Most divers don't make it this far out in the Keys,
but if you're looking for a day of diving as a break from
the nonstop party in Old Town, expect to pay about $45

and upward for a two-tank dive. Serious divers can book dive trips to the Dry Tortugas.

Operating nearly 40 years, **Dive Key West** (⊠ *3128 N. Roosevelt Blvd., Key West* ☎ *305/296–3823* ⊕ *www.divekeywest. com*) is a full-service dive center that has charters, instruction, gear rental, sales, and repair. Snorkel trips range from $49 to $69.

Captain's Corner (⊠ *125 Ann St.* ☎ *305/296–8865* ⊕ *www. captainscorner.com*), a PADI-certified dive shop, has classes in several languages and twice-daily snorkel and dive trips ($40–$45) to reefs and wrecks aboard the 60-foot dive boat *Sea Eagle*. Equipment rental is extra.

Debuting in 2009 and catering to cruise passengers, **Eco Scuba Key West** (⊠ *5130 Overseas Hwy., Key West* ☎ *305/851–1899* ⊕ *www.ecoscuba.com*) offers daily eco-tours plus tech diving, lobstering, snorkel, and scuba diving packages. Snorkel trips start at $89; scuba from $129.

Snorkel adventures at **Sea Bear Aquatic Adventures** (⊠ *Key West Historic Seaport, Key West* ☎ *305/304–3652* ⊕ *www. seabearkeywest.com*) combine with eco-touring in a 23-foot boat for up to six with Capt. Bernard Rasch at the helm. Snorkel tours for six start at $450.

Safely dive the coral reefs without getting a scuba certification with **Snuba of Key West** (⊠ *Garrison Bight Marina, Palm Ave. between Eaton St. and N. Roosevelt Blvd.* ☎ *305/292–4616* ⊕ *www.snubakeywest.com*). Ride out to the reef on a catamaran, then follow your guide underwater for a one-hour tour of the coral reefs. You wear a regulator with a breathing hose that is attached to a floating air tank on the surface. No prior diving or snorkeling experience is necessary, but you must know how to swim. The $99 price includes beverages.

TOURING

AIR TOURS

Island Aeroplane Tours (⊠ *Key West Airport, 3469 S. Roosevelt Blvd.* ☎ *305/294–8687 or 877/359–5397* ⊕ *www. keywestairtours.com*) flies up to two passengers in a 1941 Waco, an open-cockpit biplane; tours range from an eight-minute overview of Key West ($60 for two) to a 45-minute reef and wreck excursion ($295 for two).

BIKE TOURS

Lloyd's Original Tropical Bike Tour (✉ *Truman Ave. and Simonton St., Key West* ☎ *305/304–4700* ⊕ *www.lloydstropical-biketour.com*), led by a 30-year Key West veteran, explores the natural, noncommercial side of Key West at a leisurely pace, stopping on backstreets and in backyards of private homes to sample native fruits and view indigenous plants and trees; at City Cemetery; and at the Medicine Garden, a private meditation garden. The behind-the-scenes tours run two hours and cost $37, including bike rental.

BOAT TOURS

Dancing Dolphin Spirit Charters (✉ *MM 5 OS at Murray's Marina, 5710 U.S. 1, Key West* ☎ *305/304–7562 or 888/822–7366* ⊕ *www.captainvictoria.com*) offers eco-tours that frequently include encounters with wild dolphins. While island-hopping, you visit underwater gardens, natural shoreline, and mangrove habitats. For her Dolphin Day for Humans tour, she pulls you through the water, equipped with mask and snorkel, on a specially designed "dolphin water massage board." Sometimes dolphins follow the boat and swim among participants. Tours also include Sacred Sound Healing Retreats, a self-transformational retreat using vibrations and sounds. All equipment is supplied. Tours leave from Murray's Marina.

For something with more of an adrenaline boost, book with **White Knuckle Thrill Boat Ride** (✉ *Sunset Marina, 5555 College Rd., Key West* ☎ *305/797–0459* ⊕ *www.whiteknucklethrillboatride.com*). The speedboat holds up to 12 people for doing 360s, fishtails, and other on-the-water stunts in the Gulf. The cost is $59 per person.

BUS TOURS

The **Conch Tour Train** (✉ *Key West* ☎ *305/294–5161 or 888/916–8687* ⊕ *www.conchtrain.com*) is a 90-minute narrated tour of Key West, traveling 14 mi through Old Town and around the island. Board at Mallory Square or Angela Street and Duval Street depot every half-hour (9–4:35 from Mallory Square). The cost is $29 (go online for discounted tickets).

Old Town Trolley (✉ *201 Front St., Key West* ☎ *305/296–6688 or 888/910–8687* ⊕ *www.trolleytours.com*) operates trolley-style buses, departing from the Mallory Square and Roosevelt Boulevard depots every 30 minutes (9–4:30 from Mallory Square, later at other stops), for 90-minute narrated tours of Key West. The smaller trolleys go places the larger Conch Tour Train won't fit. You may disembark at any of 12 stops and reboard a later trolley. The cost is $29, but you can save a little by booking online. It also offers package deals with Old Town attractions.

In 2010, **City View Trolley Tours** (✉ *Key West* ☎ *305/294–0644* ⊕ *www.cityviewtrolleys.com*) began service, offering a little competition to the Conch Train and Old Town Trolley, which are owned by the same company. Its rates are more affordable at $19 per adult. Tours depart every 30 minutes from 9:30-4:30. Passengers can board and disembark at any of nine stops, and can reboard at will.

Key West Business Guild's (✉ *513 Truman Ave.* ✉ *Box 1208, Key West 33041* ☎ *305/294–4603 or 800/535–7797* ⊕ *www.gaykeywestfl.com*) 75-minute Gay & Lesbian Historic Trolley Tours highlight the contributions gay and lesbian writers, artists, politicians, designers, and celebrities have made to Key West's past. Tours, which cost $25, depart Saturday at 11 AM from 604 Simonton Street. Look for the rainbow flags on the trolley.

WALKING TOURS

In addition to publishing several good guides on Key West, **Historic Florida Keys Foundation** (✉ *510 Greene St., Old City Hall, Key West* ☎ *305/292–6718*) conducts tours of the City Cemetery Tuesday and Thursday at 9:30.

The **Historic Key West Walking Tour** (✉ *1 Whitehead St., Mallory Square, Key West* ☎ *305/292–8990* ⊕ *www.trusted-tours.com*) departs two to three times daily from the Key West Shipwreck Treasures Museum in Mallory Square, and takes in nearly two hours' worth of Old Town sights for $18 per adult.

Key West's Ghosts & Legends Haunted Tour (✉ *Tours meet at Duval and Caroline Sts.* ✉ *Box 1807, Charleston, SC 29402* ☎ *305/294–1713 or 866/622–4467* ⊕ *www.keywestghosts.com*) offers nightly tours at 7 and 9 ($18), including a visit to the Old City Morgue, haunted Victorian mansions, and the Key West Cemetery to hear fascinating and sometimes bone-chilling stories of real-life events and people. Tours meet at Duval and Caroline streets. Reservations are required.

For a more spectacular spiritual experience, tag along with **The Original Ghost Tour's** (✉ *430 Duval St., Key West* ☎ *305/294–9255* ⊕ *www.hauntedtours.com*) 90-minute, lantern-led stroll around Old Town. It departs nightly from the Crowne Plaza La Concha Hotel at 430 Duval Street, and costs $15.

SHOPPING

On these streets you'll find colorful local art of widely varying quality, key limes made into everything imaginable, and the raunchiest T-shirts in the civilized world. Browsing the boutiques—with frequent pub stops along the way—makes for an entertaining stroll down Duval Street. Cocktails certainly help the appreciation of some goods, such as the figurine of a naked man blowing bubbles out his backside or the swashbuckling pirate costumes that are not just for Halloween anymore.

Where to start? **Bahama Village** is an enclave of spruced-up shops, restaurants, and vendors responsible for the restoration of the colorful historic district where Bahamians settled in the 19th century. The village lies roughly between Whitehead and Fort streets and Angela and Catherine streets. Hemingway frequented the bars, restaurants, and boxing rings in this part of town.

ARTS AND CRAFTS

Key West is filled with art galleries, and the variety is truly amazing. Most of them congregate around the south end of Duval Street. Much is locally produced by the town's large artist community, but many galleries carry international artists from as close as Haiti and as far away as France. Local artists do a great job of preserving the island's architecture and spirit.

★ At **Alan S. Maltz Gallery** (⊠ *1210 Duval St.* ☎ *305/294–0005* ⊕ *www.alanmaltz.com*) the owner, declared the state's official wildlife photographer by the Wildlife Foundation of Florida, captures the state's nature and character in stunning portraits. Spend four figures for large-format images on canvas or save on small prints and close-outs.

Art@830 (⊠ *830 Caroline St., Historic Seaport* ☎ *305/295– 9595* ⊕ *www.art830.com*) carries a little bit of everything, from pottery to paintings. Most outstanding is its selection of glass art, particularly the jellyfish lamps.

Cuba, Cuba! (⊠ *814 Duval St.* ☎ *305/295–9442 or 800/621– 3596* ⊕ *cubacubastore.com*) stocks paintings, sculptures, and photos by Cuban artists.

The **Gallery on Greene** (⊠ *606 Greene St.* ☎ *305/294–1669* ⊕ *www.galleryongreene.com*) showcases politically incorrect art by Jeff MacNelly and three-dimensional paintings by Mario Sanchez. This is the largest gallery–exhibition space in Key West.

The oldest private art gallery in Key West, **Gingerbread Square Gallery** (⊠ *1207 Duval St.* ☎ *305/296–8900* ⊕ *www. gingerbreadsquaregallery.com*) represents local and internationally acclaimed artists on an annually changing basis, in mediums ranging from graphics to art glass.

Glass Reunions (⊠ *825 Duval St.* ☎ *305/294–1720* ⊕ *www. glassreunions.com*) showcases a collection of wild and impressive fine-art glass. It's worth a stop just to see the imaginative and over-the-top glass chandeliers, jewelry, dishes, and platters.

Haitian-art connoisseurs will love the bright colors in the paintings, the bead-and-sequin work in the handicrafts, and fine metal sculptures at the **Haitian Art Company** (⊠ *1100 Truman Ave.* ☎ *305/296–8932* ⊕ *www.haitian-art-co.com*).

Historian, photographer, and painter Sharon Wells opened **KW Light Gallery** (⊠ *1203 Duval St.* ☎ *305/294–0566* ⊕ *www. kwlightgallery.com*) to showcase her own fine-art photography and painted tiles and canvases, as well as the works of other national artists. You can find historic photos here as well.

Lucky Street Gallery (⊠ *1130 Duval St.* ☎ *305/294–3973*) sells high-end contemporary paintings. There are also a few pieces of jewelry by internationally recognized Key West–based artists. Changing exhibits, artist receptions, and special events make this a lively venue.

Pelican Poop Shoppe (⊠ *314 Simonton St.* ☎ *305/296–3887* ⊕ *www.pelicanpoopshoppe.com*) sells Caribbean art in a historic building with Hemingway connections. For $2 or a $10 purchase, you can stroll the tropical courtyard garden. The owners buy directly from the artisans every year, so the prices are very attractive.

Potters Charles Pearson and Timothy Roeder can be found at **Whitehead St. Pottery** (⊠ *322 Julia St.* ☎ *305/294–5067* ⊕ *www.whiteheadstreetpottery.com*), where they display their porcelain stoneware and raku-fired vessels. The setting, around two koi ponds with a burbling fountain, is as sublime as the art.

BOOKS

The **Key West Island Bookstore** (⊠ *513 Fleming St.* ☎ *305/294–2904*) is a home away from home for the large Key West writers' community. It carries new, used, and rare titles. It specializes in Hemingway, Tennessee Williams, and South Florida mystery writers.

CIGARS

At **Conch Republic Cigar Factory** (⊠ *512 Greene St.* ☎ *305/295–9036 or 800/317–2167* ⊕ *www.conch-cigars.com*) a cigar-roller demonstrates hand-rolling techniques. The shop sells flavored and unflavored varieties.

CLOTHING AND FABRICS

Don't leave town without a browse through the legendary **Fairvilla Megastore** (⊠ *520 Front St.* ☎ *305/292–0448* ⊕ *www.fairvilla.com*), where you'll find an astonishing array of fantasy wear, outlandish costumes (check out the pirate section), and other interesting souvenirs.

A pair of **Kino Sandals** (⊠ *107 Fitzpatrick St.* ☎ *305/294–5044* ⊕ *www.kinosandalfactory.com* ⊘ *Closed Sun. in off-season*) was once a public declaration that you'd been to Key West. The attraction? You can watch these inexpensive items being made. The factory has been churning out several styles since 1966. Walk up to the counter, grab a pair, try them on, and lay down some cash. It's that simple.

Take home a shopping bag full of scarlet hibiscus, fuchsia heliconias, blue parrot fish, or pink flamingo fabric from the **Seam Shoppe** (⊠ *1114 Truman Ave.* ☎ *305/296–9830* ⊕ *www.tropicalfabricsonline.com*), which has the city's widest selection of tropical-print fabrics.

The surf is definitely not up in Key West, but the surfer attitude is. **Shirley Can't Surf** (⊠ *624 Duval St.* ☎ *305/292–1009*) is crammed with surf wear, including its own brand T-shirts proclaiming this the southernmost surf shop since 1965. It also stocks skateboarding equipment.

Get beach ready with colorful towels from **Towels of Key West** (⊠ *806 Duval St.* ☎ *305/292–1120 or 800/927–0316* ⊕ *www.towelsofkeywest.net*). There are more than 60 unique towel designs, some you'd expect, others more whimsical. All are hand-sewn on the island.

FOOD AND DRINK

★ The **Blond Giraffe** (✉ *802 Duval St.* ☎ *305/293–7874* ✉ *614 Front St.* ☎ *305/296–2020* ✉ *1209 Truman Ave.* ☎ *305/295– 6776* ⊕ *www.blondgiraffe.com*) turned an old family recipe for key lime pie into one of the island's success stories. Its five Key West locations are known for a pie with delicate pastry, sweet-tart custard filling, and thick meringue topping. The key lime rum cake is the best-selling product for shipping home, and even more decadent grilled and topped with vanilla ice cream and chocolate sauce. For a snack on the run, try the frozen chocolate-dipped pie on a stick.

Fausto's Food Palace (✉ *522 Fleming St.* ☎ *305/296–5663* ✉ *1105 White St.* ☎ *305/294–5221*) is a market in the traditional town-square sense. Since 1926 Fausto's has been the spot to catch up on the week's gossip and to chill out in summer—it has groceries, organic foods, marvelous wines, a sushi chef on duty from 8 AM to 6 PM, and box lunches to go.

★ In recent years, **Kermit's Key West Lime Shoppe** (✉ *200 Elizabeth St., Historic Seaport* ☎ *305/296–0806 or 800/376– 0806* ⊕ *www.keylimeshop.com*) has replaced Blond Giraffe in the hearts of many locals. You'll see Kermit himself standing on the corner every time a trolley passes, pie in hand. Besides pie, his shop carries a multitude of key lime products from barbecue sauce to jellybeans. His pre-frozen pies, dressed with a special long-lasting whipped cream instead of meringue, travels well.

You'll be pleasantly surprised with the fruit wines sold at the **Key West Winery** (✉ *103 Simonton St.* ☎ *305/292–1717 or 866/880–1717* ⊕ *www.thekeywestwinery.com*). Display crates hold bottles of wines made from blueberries, blackberries, pineapples, cherries, mangoes, watermelons, tomatoes, and, of course, key limes. Stop in for a free tasting.

If you like it hot, you'll love **Peppers of Key West** (✉ *602 Greene St.* ☎ *305/295–9333 or 800/597–2823* ⊕ *www. peppersofkeywest.com*). The shop has hundreds of sauces, salsas, and sweets guaranteed to light your fire.

GIFTS AND SOUVENIRS

Part museum, part shopping center, **Cayo Hueso y Habana** (✉ *410 Wall St., Mallory Sq.* ☎ *305/293–7260*) occupies a circa-1879 warehouse with a hand-rolled-cigar shop, one-of-a-kind souvenirs, a Cuban restaurant, wood carvings by

Mario Sanchez, and exhibits that tell of the island's Cuban heritage. Outside, a memorial garden pays homage to the island's Cuban ancestors.

★ **Fast Buck Freddie's** (✉ *500 Duval St.* ☎ *305/294–2007* ⊕ *www. fastbuckfreddies.com*) sells a classy, hip selection of gifts, including every flamingo item imaginable. It has a whole department called "Tropical Trash," and carries such imaginative items as an electric fan in the shape of a rooster.

For that unique (but slightly overpriced) souvenir of your trip to Key West, head to **Montage** (✉ *512 Duval St.* ☎ *305/395–9101 or 877/396–4278* ⊕ *montagekeywest. com*), where you'll discover hundreds of handcrafted signs of popular Key West guesthouses, inns, hotels, restaurants, bars, and streets. If you can't find what you're looking for, they'll make it for you.

HEALTH AND BEAUTY

Key West Aloe (✉ *419 Duval St., at Simonton St.* ☎ *305/293– 1885 or 800/445–2563* ⊕ *keywestaloe.com*) was founded in a garage in 1971. Today it produces some 1,000 perfume, sunscreen, and skin-care products for men and women.

EXCURSION TO DRY TORTUGAS NATIONAL PARK

70 mi southwest of Key West.

GETTING HERE AND AROUND

For now, two ferry boats, the *Yankee Freedom II* and the *Sunny Days Fast Cat* depart from marinas in Old Town and do day trips to Garden Key. Key West Seaplane Adventures has half- and full-day trips to the Dry Tortugas, where you can explore Fort Jefferson, built in 1846, and snorkel on the beautiful protected reef. Departing from the Key West airport, the flights include soft drinks and snorkel equipment for $249 half-day, $435 full-day, plus there's a $5 park fee. If you want to explore the park's other keys, look into renting a boat or hiring a private charter. *For more information on the two ferries and the seaplane, see the Exploring section.*

ESSENTIALS

Visitor Information Dry Tortugas National Park (⌂ *Box 6208, Key West* ☎ *305/242–7700* ⊕ *www.nps.gov/drto*).

EXPLORING

Dry Tortugas National Park covers 64,657 acres, of which only 40 acres (on seven small islands) are dry. And they're *very* dry. Lack of fresh water earned the island group part of its name back in the days of the Spanish conquistadores. The other part of the name referred to the abundance of sea turtles that then—and still today to a lesser degree—populate its waters. Diving and snorkeling these waters rate high in the logbooks of bottom-timers from around the planet.

The typical visitor from Key West, however, makes it no farther than the waters of Garden Key. Home to 19th-century Fort Jefferson, it is the destination for seaplane and fast ferry tours out of Key West. With 2½ to 6½ hours to spend on the island, visitors have time to tour the mammoth fort-come-prison and then cool off with mask and snorkel along the fort's moat wall.

History buffs might remember long-deactivated Fort Jefferson, the largest brick building in the western hemisphere, as the prison that held Dr. Samuel Mudd, who unwittingly set John Wilkes Booth's leg after the assassination of Abraham Lincoln. Three other men were also held there for complicity in the assassination. Original construction on the fort began in 1846 and continued for 30 years, but was never completed because the invention of the rifled cannon made it obsolete. That's when it became a Civil War prison and later a wildlife refuge. In 1935 President Franklin Roosevelt declared it a national monument for its historic and natural value.

The brick fort acts as a gigantic, almost 16-acre reef. Around its moat walls, coral grows and schools of snapper, grouper, and wrasses hang out. To reach the offshore coral heads requires about 15 minutes of swimming over sea-grass beds. The reef formations blaze with the color and majesty of brain coral, swaying sea fans, and flitting tropical fish. It takes a bit of energy to swim the distance, but the water depth pretty much measures under 7 feet all the way, allowing for sandy spots to stop and rest. (Standing in sea-grass meadows and on coral is detrimental to marine life.)

Serious snorkelers and divers head out farther offshore to epic formations, including Palmata Patch, one of the few surviving concentrations of elkhorn coral in the Keys. Day-trippers congregate on the sandy beach to relax in the sun and enjoy picnics. Overnight tent campers have use of restroom facilities and achieve a total getaway from noise, lights, and civilization in general. Remember that no matter how you get here, the park's $5 admission fee must be paid in cash.

The park has set up with signage a self-guided tour that takes about 45 minutes. You should budget more time if you're into photography, because the scenic shots are hard to pass up. Ranger-guided tours are also available at certain times. Check in at the visitor center for a schedule. The small office also shows an orientation video, sells books and other educational materials, and, most importantly, provides a blast of air-conditioning on hot days.

Birders in the know bring binoculars to watch some 100,000 nesting sooty terns at their only U.S. nesting site, Bush Key, adjacent to Garden Key. Noddy terns also nest in the spring. During winter migrations, birds fill the airspace so thickly they literally fall from the sky to make their pit stops, birders say. More than 300 species have been spotted in the park's seven islands, including frigatebirds, boobies, cormorants, and white-tailed tropic birds. Bush Key is closed to foot traffic during nesting season, January through September. ✍ *Box 6208, Key West* ☎ *305/242–7700* ⊕ *www. nps.gov/drto.*

Yankee Freedom II. If you want to save some money or have a fear of small planes, consider this fast catamaran. The ferry to Dry Tortugas National Park takes 2¼ hours each way. The time passes quickly on the uncramped vessel (it holds 250 passengers, but limits its trip to 100). It's equipped with three restrooms, two freshwater showers, and two bars (open on return trip only). Stretch out on two decks: one an air-conditioned salon with cushioned seating, the other an open sundeck with sunny and shaded seating. You can also spot the same creatures and wrecks visible from the seaplane tour, albeit with a less impressive view. Continental breakfast and lunch are included. On arrival at Garden Key, a naturalist leads a 40-minute guided tour, followed by lunch and a free afternoon for swimming, snorkeling, and exploring. The tour allows you approximately 4½ hours on Garden Key, and generally gets you back to Key West by 5:30, in time for Sunset Celebration. The vessel is ADA-certified for visitors using wheelchairs. ✉ *Lands End Marina, 240 Margaret St., Key West* ☎ *305/294–7009 or*

800/634–0939 ⊕ *www.yankeefreedom.com* ⊠ *$160* ⊙ *Trips daily at 8* AM.

Sunny Days Fast Cat. Smaller and more economical, the *Sunny Day Fast Cat* follows pretty much the same schedule as the ferry, and includes the same perks, but promises a more stable and slightly speedier ride aboard its sleek, lighter catamaran. Guests can roam the air-conditioned cabin and rear sundeck and can use a freshwater shower once back on board. Camping transportation rates are about $30 higher per person. ⊠ *Historic Key West Seaport, Greene and Elizabeth Sts., Key West* ☎ *305/292–6100 or 800/236–7937* ⊕ *www.drytortugasferry.com* ⊠ *$145* ⊙ *Trips daily at 7* AM.

Key West Seaplane Adventures. The 35- to 40-minute trip to the Dry Tortugas skims above the trademark windowpane-clear waters of the Florida Keys. The seaplane perspective provides an awesome experience that could result in a stiff neck from craning to look out the window and down from 500 feet above. In the Flats that edge Key West, you can spot stingrays, sea turtles, and sharks in the shallow water. In the area dubbed The Quicksands, water plunges to 30-foot depths and sand undulates in dune-like formations. Shipwrecks also festoon these waters; here's where Mel Fisher harvested treasure from the *Atocha* and *Margarita.* His 70-foot work ship, the *Arbutus,* deteriorated and eventually sank at the northern edge of the treasure sites. With its mast poking out above water, it's easy to spot and fun to photograph. From there, the water deepens from emerald hues to shades of deep blue as depths reach 70 feet. Seaplanes of Key West's most popular trip is the half-day option, where you spend about 2½ hours on Garden Key. The seaplanes leave during your stay, so be prepared to carry all of your possessions with you. The half-day tour costs $249 per person. The morning trip beats the ferries to the island, so you'll have it to yourself until the others arrive. Snorkeling equipment, soft drinks, and birding lists are supplied. ⊠ *Key West International Airport, 3471 S. Roosevelt Blvd., Key West* ☎ *305/293–9300* ⊕ *www. keywestseaplanecharters.com.*

DID YOU KNOW? The Dry Tortugas lies in the Central Time Zone. Key West Seaplane pilots like to tell their passengers that they land 15 minutes before they take off.

WHERE TO STAY

⚠ **Dry Tortugas National Park.** A cluster of trees and a foundation of sand define the park's small camping area. The grounds aren't very private during the day, but after the seaplanes and ferries leave, it doesn't get more peaceful anywhere on this earth. Its eight sites each accommodate six people and three tents. Costing $3 per person per night, they are available on a first-come, first-served basis. There's also a group site available to for up to 40 people (15 tents) with advance reservations. Note that there's no water available, and campers must carry off whatever they bring onto the island. No open fires are allowed, only camp stoves and charcoal briquettes used in the grills. Pack your food carefully to keep it safe from the island's controlled rat population. Restrooms are locked from 10 to 3, but campers are allowed to use facilities aboard the ferries. ♿ *Picnic tables, grills, swimming (ocean)* ⇨ *8 tent sites* 🏕 *Dry Tortugas National Park, Garden Key, Box 6208, Key West* ☎ *305/242–7700 (group site reservations)* ⊕ *www.nps.gov/drto* 🖃 *$3.*

Gateways to the Keys

6

WORD OF MOUTH

"The Keys are definitely a get out on the water type place instead of a driving up and down U.S. 1 kind of place. Bars and restaurants open early and close early. Get out over the water. That is where the most amazing things in the Keys are."

—GoTravel

ALTHOUGH IT'S POSSIBLE TO FLY INTO KEY WEST, most people don't because of the expense and because of the limited number of flights. Furthermore, if you are visiting the Upper or Middle Keys, there is a drive regardless of which airport you fly into. This means that most visitors flying into Florida to visit the Keys will pass through Miami. In many cases, people choose to stay a while to absorb some of the new luxe hotels, hot nightlife, and stylish restaurants, not to mention the expansive beaches, of which the Keys do not have an abundance. Travelers on more of a budget may want to look a bit farther afield to either Homestead or Florida City, both south of Miami, the two major gateways to both the Keys and the Everglades.

See ⇨ **Travel Smart Florida Keys** for information on flights and car rentals in Miami.

RESTAURANTS

Miami has a vibrant dining scene, with prices to match, but you can still find reasonably priced local restaurants and chains, but mostly outside the trendy South Beach area. Most restaurants south of Miami are small mom-and-pop establishments serving home-style food or local specialties such as alligator, fish, stone crab, frogs' legs, and fresh Florida lobster from the Keys. There are plenty of chain restaurants and fast-food establishments, especially in the Homestead and Florida City areas.

WHAT IT COSTS				
¢	$	$$	$$$	$$$$
RESTAURANTS				
under $10	$10–$15	$15–$20	$20–$30	over $30
HOTELS				
under $80	$80–$100	$100–$140	$140–$220	over $220

Restaurant prices are per person for a main course at dinner. Hotel prices are for a standard double room, excluding 7%–7.7% sales tax (depending on the county) and 5%–6% tourist/bed tax.